SERIAL KILLERS

SERIAL KILLERS

The Insatiable Passion

David Lester, PhD

The Charles Press, Publishers

Philadelphia

The Charles Press, Publishers
Post Office Box 15715
Philadelphia, Pennsylvania 19103

(215) 496-9616 - Telephone
(215) 496-9637 - Fax
mailbox@charlespresspub.com
http://www.charlespresspub.com

7 9 11 12 10 8

Library of Congress Cataloging-in-Publication Data

Lester, David, 1942-
Serial killers: the insatiable passion / David Lester.
p. cm.
Includes bibliographical references and index.
ISBN 0-914783-77-7
1. Serial murders. 2. Serial murderers. 3. Serial murderers - Case studies.
I. Title.
HV6505.L47 1995
364.1'523 — dc20   95-19309
CIP

Printed in the United States of America

Contents

Preface

Serial killers have always fascinated and horrified society. It has only been since the early 1970s, however, that this specific type of criminal was defined as murderers who methodically slay a succession of people (three or more) over a period of time (at least 30 days). This is not to say that serial killers have not always existed. They have since ancient times. But until recently, there has been little research and even less understanding of who these people are and why they kill.

Despite the enormous amount of coverage of serial killers in the news media, in movies and books and on television, until now there have been few, if any, reliable sources of information about them. Most everyone takes a sensationalist approach to the subject, and who could blame them; the crimes of Jeffrey Dahmer and John Wayne Gacy do not lend themselves easily to rational analysis. In taking this type of approach, however, the motives and reasons behind the crimes tend to be lost among the gory details. It is these important but rarely explained areas that will be the focus of this book.

The first step in this analysis is to establish whether there is a solid, useable profile of the serial killer. By looking at many types of serial killers from many different eras, we will try to discover what these murderers have in common and what characteristics, if any, they share. It is also necessary to examine the reasons for this type of behavior. What drives these people to kill and to kill again, never stopping until they are caught? What need could be so great that it would override all sense of personal conscience or social respectability?

In attempting to answer these questions, we will also explore the lives of a few of the more notable serial killers and the cultures in which they existed. Can any motives be found to help us understand what made them act the way they did? To simply dismiss serial killers as insane is a grave mistake. Indeed, an overwhelming number are not insane. Of those who have been caught in the last several decades, very few, if any, have been able to successfully claim that they were insane. To the contrary, they are careful, deliberate killers who are well aware of what they are doing and know that killing is wrong.

It is this analytical approach that has been so lacking in the majority of treatments of serial killers. Therefore, in this book, it is my intention to take a comprehensive look at the psychological and sociological aspects of the perpetrators of this most gruesome behavior. The fact that these killers exist anonymously in society, their actions going unnoticed until it is too late, makes it all the more necessary that their motives be understood. It is simply not enough to look at the details surrounding serial killers; we must look beyond the killing act into the passion that drives them.

David Lester, PhD

SERIAL KILLERS

PART I

FACTS AND THEORIES

Chapter 1

Murder in America

To understand the phenomenon of serial murder in America, it is first necessary to have some information about murder in general. For example, in order to appreciate the fact that serial murder appears to be more common in America than in other industrialized nations, one must know that murder *in general* is more common in America than in other industrialized nations. In this first chapter, then, we will examine some of the facts and theories about murder in America (cf. Lester, 1991).

The Epidemiology of Murder

The homicide rate in America has been high throughout this century. In 1935, the rate was 8.5 people per 100,000 people per year. It dropped to 4.5 in 1955, rose to 10.7 in 1980, and has dropped a little since then, ranging now from 8 to 9 per 100,000. Thus, although the American public and American politicians seem particularly concerned about murder today, the rate is not particularly high given America's past.

There is also concern about the large number of murderers who remain unidentified and therefore not captured. In 1989, the clearance rate for murder was 68 percent—far higher than for other crimes (for example, 52 percent of rapes and 14 percent of burglaries are cleared).

Homicide rates vary across America, typically being much higher in the South and West. For example, in 1994, homicide rates ranged from 1.7 in New Hampshire and 2.1 in North Dakota to 18.4 in Texas and 17.2 in Nevada.

For the period 1992 to 1994, America's homicide rate was 11.6 compared to 1.7 in Australia, 1.6 in Italy, and 0.6 in England and Wales. The nations that had higher homicide rates were mostly all

3

located in Central and South America: for example, 36.3 in Colombia, 18.2 in Mexico and 10.8 in Brazil. Outside of the Americas, only South Africa, Thailand and Zimbabwe had higher rates. In general, nations with a higher quality of life have lower homicide rates (and higher suicide rates).

In America, the majority of murders are committed with a firearm (64 percent in 1994), and the majority of firearm murders are committed using a handgun (78 percent in 1994). The risk of being murdered peaks for those aged 20 to 24 years of age (21.6 in 1994), particularly for men, but has a secondary peak for the murder of babies in their first year of life (7.6 in 1994). Most murders are between people of the same race (86 percent in 1994). The murder rate is higher in urban areas than in rural areas.

Murder rates are higher on weekends (presumably because people at leisure drink, argue, and on rare occasions murder one another), are higher on national holidays such as Labor Day and Christmas Day, but show no seasonal variation or association with the weather and the phase of the moon.

The Murderers

Men murder at a higher rate than women and African Americans murder at a higher rate than white Americans. For example, in the city of Philadelphia between the years 1948 and 1952, the murder rates (per 100,000 per year) were:

African American males	41.7
African American females	9.3
white males	3.4
white females	0.4

Some murderers commit suicide after murdering, but this is rare. The rate in America is about 0.2 per 100,000 per year (compared to a total murder rate of about 9). People who murder relatives or lovers are more likely to commit suicide, as are mothers who murder their children. Murder-suicide pacts in which one person kills the other with that person's consent and then commits suicide are very rare, accounting for no more than 0.7 percent of all suicides.

The Victims

As we have noted above, victims tend to resemble murderers in several ways. Typically, they are the same age and the same race. However, men murder men more than women murder men, and men murder women more than women murder women. Similar proportions of murderers and victims are intoxicated at the time of the murder, and they have similar criminal histories.

The most common relationship between murderer and victim is friend or acquaintance (38 percent in 1984), followed by relatives (18 percent) and strangers (18 percent), and 26 percent are undetermined.

In some situations, victims are found to have played a triggering role in the events that led to their own murder; this is called *victim-precipitated homicide*. For example, a person may start the fight that causes his death. In one study of murders in Philadelphia, Wolfgang (1958) found that the victim had played some role in about 25 percent of the murders that occurred. Interest in this phenomenon has led to the growth in recent years of a new scholarly discipline called *victimology*.

The Media

The most common forms of murder we read about in the press or hear about on television are mass serial murders, assassinations of national figures, gangland or professional killings, murder where the victim or the murderer is a prominent person, any murder with bizarre overtones, murders with political implications and murders which raise issues about the criminal justice system. Cain (1982), who worked for *The Detroit News*, noted that these categories of murder constitute only about 5 percent of all of the murders which occur in America. Thus, the murders we hear about through the media are far from typical.

Theories of Murder

There are many hypotheses about what causes people to murder, but few have been adequately tested by empirical research so that they can be confirmed or disconfirmed. Thus, although this section is titled "Theories of Murder," a better title may be "Speculations About the Causes of Murder." Let us look at the contributions of the different scholarly disciplines to the understanding of murder.

Physiological Theories

Very little is known about the genetics of violence. In the 1960s, there was initial excitement over the discovery of an increased frequency of a chromosomal abnormality in men incarcerated in mental-penal institutions (institutions for the criminally insane) labeled XYY because of the presence of an extra sex chromosome. Whereas about 0.01 percent of newborn boys have this defect, about 2 percent of the male inmates of mental-penal institutions have the same defect. XYY men tend to have larger body sizes and they are less intelligent and have a greater likelihood of abnormal electrical activity in the brain than normal men. It is felt by some that these mediating factors caused them to turn to criminal behavior and eventually to be sentenced to a mental-penal institution. However, the vast majority of XYY men are law-abiding, and the XYY defect can contribute to an explanation of only an occasional murder.

Abnormal electrical activity in the brain, indicative of brain damage, is found in about 24 percent of murderers as compared to about 12 percent of normal people. However, about 65 percent of habitually aggressive assaulters have abnormal electrical activity in the brain, a much higher percentage than for murderers. The brain damage may be genetically caused or a result of prior trauma to the head. Incidentally, there is no evidence that epileptics, who are subject to periodic brain seizures, have an increased risk of becoming murderers.

Mark and Ervin (1970) studied a woman who had made unprovoked attacks on others. In one instance she attacked and killed a stranger in the rest room at a theater. The researchers recorded abnormal electrical activity in her amygdalae (subcortical structures in the brain) during periods when she snarled and acted fiercely angry, even if she was in a room by herself. Removal of both amygdalae eliminated her violent behavior.

When examining a murderer, mental health professionals rarely monitor the electrical activity in the brain, but commonly inquire about "soft signs" of brain damage, such as episodes of losing conscious for any reason, involvement in car crashes, oxygen deprivation during birth, seizures and migraine or cluster headaches.

Some scholars, particularly those who call themselves sociobiologists, are convinced that aggression is an "instinct" found in every species, including humans. The problem, then, is to channel this aggressive instinct into socially acceptable outlets, such as contact sports for example, rather than letting it out in vicious behavior such as fighting and possibly assault or murder. However, this hypothesis clearly does not explain why only a very few people turn to murder to express their aggression. It does suggest that murderers fail to find socially acceptable outlets for their aggression, and even though it implies that nonmurderers do have socially acceptable outlets, there are certainly many people who do not and certainly not all of these people become murderers. Nevertheless, there is some evidence for this hypothesis. Palmer (1960), for example, found that murderers had indeed found fewer socially acceptable outlets for their anger than their nonmurdering brothers.

Psychological Theories

Although murderers occasionally claim that they were not responsible for their murderous acts because they say they were "insane," there is no evidence that the incidence of murder is greater among people with psychiatric disorders than among normal people. In the United States, most people with psychiatric disorders, although they may behave eccentrically, tend to be as law-abiding as the rest of us. This is not necessarily the case in other nations. In Europe, for example, a fair percentage of murderers are seriously psychiatrically disturbed, but murder in Europe is not a common occurrence. In America, however, where murder is much more common, the vast majority of murderers are not seriously psychiatrically disturbed.

It has been argued that the experience of severe frustration in childhood and adolescence builds up a reservoir of anger toward others that may later result in violent acts, including murder. Palmer (1960), in a comparison of murderers with nonmurderers, found that the murderers had experienced twice as many traumas during childhood and adolescence as nonmurderers. These traumas included suffering difficult births, serious operations and illnesses, major accidents, congenital or acquired deformities, physical beatings by persons other than parents, and being subject to very strict discipline and uncaring mothers. They also were more likely to be bed-wetters and stutterers to have difficulties in school, symptoms that indicate a high level of frustration and stress which, in turn, result in additional frustration and stress.

Palmer gave as an example the case of an adolescent we shall call Mike who murdered a middle-aged prostitute when he was 18. He had just had intercourse with her and then tried to rob her. As this was happening, Mike remembered all the horrible things that had happened to him in his past: he was constantly beaten; at age five, his uncle got angry at him and threw him against a stove; his two older brothers beat him with branches until he was covered with welts, making him unconscious for two days; his uncle put him under the hood of a car and started the engine; his uncle and brothers gave him electric shocks; his brothers threw him in a stream to teach him to swim, and nearly drowned him; they tied a snake around his neck, a trauma so intense it took him a week to recover; and they threw a homemade javelin into his leg. Often, a child who has been subject to this kind of torture, grows up to be furious with his mother for failing to protect him from such abuse. Perhaps Mike saw the middle-aged woman he murdered as a substitute for his mother and he took his rage out on her.

Megargee (1966) proposed a typology of murderers based on their ability to control aggressive impulses. *Undercontrolled* murderers have little control over their aggressive impulses; if someone frustrates, irritates or insults them, they aggress immediately. Thus, they are continually in fights, not surprisingly, and such fights occasionally result in the death of the frustrator. *Overcontrolled* murderers, on the other hand, have learned to inhibit any expression of their anger. Thus, when frustrated, they block any outward sign of their anger and may often be entirely unconscious of doing this. Eventually, this unexpressed anger builds up until one additional frustration releases all of the years of pent-up rage. The result is often a brutal murder, typically of family members, in which the victims may be shot many times or stabbed over and over again.

A Subculture of Violence

Because murder shows a strong regional variation, both within America and across the world, sociologists have proposed that a small subculture develops in some cultures in which aggression and violence become acceptable and even the norm. For example, in America, the South is thought by some to have a violent subculture, characterized by high rates of murder, high rates of gun ownership and strongly conservative political attitudes. The high rates of violence and murder among adolescent gangs today can be seen as another example of small, volatile subcultures developing in many cities across America.

It might be argued that America as a whole has a *culture* of violence. Holmes and De Burger (1988) noted many features of American society that contribute to the propensity for violence (and, in the extreme, murder), including:

1. the high frequency and acceptance of interpersonal violence as a way of solving interpersonal conflicts
2. a strong emphasis on the desirability of comfort
3. a strong emphasis on the desirability of thrills and "highs"
4. a high level of resentment and a strong tendency to blame others for personal misfortunes
5. a large number of role models for violence in the media (especially on television and in films)
6. the anonymity and depersonalization that occurs in dense urban areas
7. the high mobility and interstate migration of people
8. the emphasis on immediate gratification

Thus, while the general public deplores violence and crime and would like lawmakers and politicians to "solve the problem," at the same time, this same general public pays to view violent films, reads books that include violence, wants to own guns in large quantities and tends to encourage their children (especially boys) to fight back when attacked.

Comment

Although there are several hypotheses about the causes of murder, as we have seen, they remain largely untested, and they are not sufficient to explain the reasons that people commit murder. Thus, before examining the phenomenon of serial murder, we must bear in mind that we do not have a sound understanding of ordinary murder at all.

References

Cain, S. Murder and the media. In B.L. Danto, J. Bruhns and A.H. Kutscher (eds.), *The Human Side of Homicide*. New York: Columbia University Press, 1982.

Holmes, R.M. and J. De Burger. *Serial Murder*. Beverly Hills, CA: Sage, 1988.

Lester, D. *Questions and Answers about Murder*. Philadelphia: The Charles Press, 1991.

Mark, V. and F. Ervin. *Violence and the Brain*. New York: Harper and Row, 1970.

Megargee, E.I. Undercontrolled and overcontrolled personality types in extreme antisocial aggression. *Psychological Monographs* 80(3):611, 1966.

Palmer, S. *A Study of Murder*. New York: Thomas Y. Crowell, 1960.

Wolfgang, M.E. *Patterns of Criminal Homicide*. Philadelphia: University of Pennsylvania Press, 1958.

Chapter 2

Defining Serial Murder

It may not seem to be too difficult a task to define serial murder, but as this chapter discusses, it is harder than one might suppose for a variety of reasons. First of all, what does the word murder mean?

Murder is a term used by the criminal justice system as distinct from the more general term *homicide*. Homicide refers to any killing of one person by another. There are several types of homicide: *excusable homicide,* in which the killing is unintentional and no blame attaches to the killer and *justifiable homicide,* in which the killing is justified by law such as when a police officer kills a felon within the guidelines established by the legal system. Cases in which blame does attach to the killer are called *first-degree murders* and this commonly refers to killings that are willful, deliberate and premeditated. *Second-degree murder* refers to a killing that is malicious (exhibiting elements of cruelty and recklessness) but not necessarily intentional. *Voluntary manslaughter* is a killing that takes place in the heat of anger and is not premeditated or committed with malice. *Involuntary manslaughter* is a killing that results from negligence on the part of the killer (such as when a drunk driver unintentionally kills a pedestrian). The term *serial murder* falls within offenses that fit the criminal justice system's definition of murder.

How Many Murders?

The term *serial* when applied to murder raises further problems. Serial implies that several murders have taken place at different times. How many must take place? Is a person a serial killer after two murders, or are more required? For example, Gleick (1993) reported the case of a couple, Karla Homolka and Paul Bernardo, who murdered two women in Canada. Two years after their wedding in June 1991 in Ontario, Canada, Paul Bernardo was arrested for a series of 19 rapes that he had committed in Ontario between 1987 and 1990. It was then discovered that just before his wedding ceremony, Bernardo had murdered a 14-year-old girl, Leslie Mahaffy, whose body was discovered on the day of the wedding ceremony. She had been sexually assaulted before her death, her body dismembered with a chain saw and her limbs embedded in concrete. Within a year, Bernardo murdered 15-year-old Kristen French, whose body was found in a ditch. She had also been sexually assaulted and probably kept alive for two weeks before her death.

After being physically abused by Bernardo, his wife, Karla Homolka, went to a lawyer and negotiated with the police. At the time of this writing, Homolka had pleaded guilty to manslaughter and had received a 12-year sentence. Bernardo was awaiting trial. The criminal justice system in Canada does not permit media reporting of the events of cases before trials and so the details of the Bernardo case are sketchy.

Do two murders make Bernardo a serial killer?[1] Do we require three, four, five or more before applying the label "serial killer"? And what about someone who commits, for example, 12 murders? Is he considered a serial killer only after the third murder? What if he had been captured after the first murder, before he had time to commit any more? This latter question suggests that the type of murder may play a role in determining whether a person is a serial murderer, as well as the future intentions of the murderer.

Holmes and Holmes (1994) suggested that a serial murder must involve at least three victims and that the time period between the first and last murders must be greater than 30 days. Thus, in the case discussed above, whether Bernardo killed Homolka's sister is critical for labeling Bernardo as a serial killer. (For the present discussion, we will employ the criteria suggested by Holmes and Holmes.)[2]

Does It Have To Be Murder?

Since the late 1970s, three persons have been killed and 23 others injured by bombs made by someone the police have named "Unabomber"[*] (Fernandez, 1993). Many of the bombs have been engraved with the initials FC (meaning "Fuck Computers") referring

---

[*] "*Una*bomber" refers to the fact that the bomber chose victims largely from *uni*versities and the *a*irline industry.

to Unabomber's hatred for computer technology, half of them delivered by mail and the other half by hand. The first bomb exploded at Northwestern University in 1978, injuring a security guard and a graduate student. The first fatality was Hugh Scrutton who died in 1985 after he picked up a booby-trapped package in the parking lot of his computer store in Sacramento, California. After a white male was spotted placing a bomb outside a computer store in Salt Lake City, the attacks stopped until 1993, at which time Charles Epstein, a geneticist at the University of California, was injured by a bomb delivered in a padded brown envelope to his home. David Gelernter, a computer scientist at Yale University, was similarly injured two days later. In December 1994, Thomas Moser, a New Jersey advertising executive, was killed as he opened a package delivered to his home that bore the return address of San Francisco State University. Then, in April 1995, Gilbert Murray, a California timber industry lobbyist, was killed when he opened a package that was mailed to his office in Sacramento. In a letter that Unabomber sent to newspapers, he stated that he would stop the killings if his manifesto against modern technology was printed.

Fifteen attacks and now three deaths have occurred by the explosion of bombs hand-delivered or sent through the mail. As of 1995, Unabomber technically became a serial murderer because he killed one more person, thereby meeting the three-deaths minimum.

The Timing of Murders

The killing of more than one person is called *multicide.* If several people are killed at the same time and place, in a single episode of violence, this is typically referred to as *mass murder.* Several scholars have suggested that three is the minimum number of victims for a murder to be called a mass murder (Holmes and De Burger, 1985; Hickey, 1991), while others have suggested that four are needed (Hazelwood and Douglas, 1980). Dietz (1986) suggests that injuring five and causing the death of at least three people should be considered mass murder.

In the mass murder that occurred at the McDonald's in San Ysidro, California in 1984, James Huberty killed 21 people and wounded 19 others in a single episode. However, some mass murderers do kill over much longer periods and sometimes at different, though usually nearby, locations.

We saw that Holmes and Holmes (1994) required a minimum 30-day period between the first and last murders for a person to be considered a serial murderer. But what if the time interval is less than 30 days? Holmes and Holmes suggested the term *spree murder* for these situations. For example, Moses Pearson drove through Georgia in April 1976, randomly murdering three people and wounding 13 more before killing himself with his gun (Holmes and De Burger, 1988).

Recidivism

Recidivism has been a well-researched phenomenon in criminology. Many offenders, including murderers, return to committing crimes after serving time in prison (Sellin, 1980). For example, Lehtinen (1979) noted that two paroled murderers from a sample of 994 studied were imprisoned subsequently for murder. Is a recidivist a serial murderer, or does serving time in prison set the murder count back to zero?

The Type of Murder

There seems to be a bias in the type of murderer who is labeled a serial murderer. The term is most commonly applied to persons who murder children and women and who also sexually assault the victims. A recent comprehensive listing of serial murderers by Holmes and Holmes (1994) included few contract killers who murder professionally for organized crime groups. Few contract murderers kill persons they are not commissioned to kill while they are carrying out a hit.

Charles Sinclair killed at least 14 coins and precious metals dealers between 1985 and 1990 (VICAP Alert, 1992). Sinclair was knowledgeable about coins and traveled around the United States visiting dealers. He would case a shop for several days and then enter the store to discuss purchases. As the store was closing, he would shoot the owner in the head once or twice, execution style. He would steal between $50,000 and $100,000 in each robbery, often taking items of value from the victim's body. Sinclair was arrested in August 1990 in Alaska and died of a heart attack while in custody in October

1990. He is not on the list provided by Holmes and Holmes. Is this because they did not know of Sinclair, or did they not view him as a serial murderer because he killed during the course of a robbery?

Hickey (1991) also noted that certain types of serial murderers are sometimes omitted from consideration, such as female serial killers. The motive behind the killing often leads some writers to exclude some killers from their compilations of serial murderers. For different reasons, different researchers have excluded the following: landlords who kill boarding home residents for their social security checks, hospital attendants who kill patients, nursing home staff who kill elderly residents and those who kill kin. Browning and Gerassi (1980) presented several cases of serial murderers who were professional criminals, members of organized crime subcultures, or who murdered for political, financial and business reasons.

Hickey (1991) noted one particular type of serial murderer who is often omitted from studies, namely those who committed mass murders during wartime. Hickey gave Dr. Joseph Mengele, the physician who directed the processing of concentration camp victims during the Second World War at Birkenow and Auschwitz, as one example. (His case is presented in Chapter 11.) Such people exist in every war—among the Khmer Rouge in Cambodia during their repressive rule in the 1970s and during the Balkan civil wars of the 1990s.

Other groups omitted from consideration often include the outlaws and gunslingers of America's early days. Although Jesse James and groups such as the Dalton Gang typically killed during robberies, we cannot be sure that they did not enjoy the killing itself. Furthermore, it is not clear whether commission of concurrent crimes should remove a murderer from the category of serial murderer. Other types often omitted include serial murderers who work for organized crime, pirates and outlaws of the past and acts resulting from political and industrial violence. For example, in Northern Ireland, the Middle East and Sri Lanka, there is a record of endemic violence, along with many serial killings. And those who believe that abortion is murder must conclude that doctors who carry out routine abortions are serial killers, despite the fact that they are operating legally.

The Thugs of India (Gee, 1988) illustrate one of the types of serial killers omitted from consideration by most scholars. In the thirteenth century, the secret order of Assassins carried out political assassinations from their base in Alamut, Syria. According to Marco Polo, they were annihilated by the Mongols in 1256. However, one theory is that some escaped to India and formed the nucleus of a group called the Thugs.[3] The members of the cult lived normal lives in the community but formed secret bands to attack unwary travelers. They strangled the victims, took their possessions to offer to Kali (the consort of the Hindu god Shiva) and disposed of the bodies in secret burial places. Many Thugs had hundreds of victims to their discredit, with one man claiming a total of 931 victims (Sleeman, 1933).

In the present book, we shall examine a variety of types of serial murderers from among the case studies that are presented later in this book.

Psychiatric Terminology

Murder committed with a sexual motivation is commonly called *lust murder*, or more pedantically *erotophonophilia* (Money, 1990). In a recent edition of the Diagnostic and Statistical Manual of the American Psychiatric Association (DSM III-R), there is a broad category called paraphilia, which covers sexually deviant behavior. One of the variants listed is *sexual sadism* which includes lust murder.[4] However, the use of such a term limits the scope of those acts from being included in the category of serial murder and the psychiatric diagnostic manual does not contain any other disorders specifically relevant to murder or serial murder.

Discussion

It should be noted that many of those who write on the topic of serial murder have similarly suggested that there are inadequate definitions for the term "serial murder." For example, Egger (1984) defined serial murder as when "one or more individuals, who in all known cases were males, commits a second and/or subsequent murder." Almost all other writers require three, four or more murders for serial murder to have occurred and they also require the specification of a time period in which the murders occurred. (Later in his definition, Egger says that the two murders must occur at different times, but most writers require a 30-day period.) Furthermore, there have been documented female serial murderers and so the reference to the gender of the individuals is incorrect. Egger goes on to include in his definition the requirement that the murderer and victim be strangers and adds that the murders are frequently committed in different geographical locations and are generally not committed for material gain. A good proportion of serial murderers have killed acquaintances and relatives and a definition *cannot* include words such as "generally" or "frequently." Egger, therefore, excludes many serial murders from his definition (including all committed by women and those of non-acquaintances) and confuses the general characteristics of serial murderers with their definition. Egger (1990) reviewed several definitions of serial murder and almost all of them included characteristics of the serial murderer in the definition, thereby restricting the term.

It is necessary to define the term serial murder without reference to the characteristics of the murderer or the victim. *Murder* refers to the unlawful killing of one person by another and *serial murder* refers to the timing and number of murders committed. Thus, a definition of serial murder must be restricted to these, and only these, elements if it is to be sound.

It might be helpful, of course, to obtain a list of *all* murderers who killed others during, say, a 5-year period in America and to list the numbers of murders each committed, the time periods between the first and the last for each of the multicides and whether other crimes were committed at the same time. Then we could use empirical data to see whether there were naturally occurring division points that we could then use to form categories. Without such data, we have had to rely on scholars making *ex cathedra* decisions about the number and the timing of murders to allow a multicide to qualify as a serial murder. A satisfactory definition of serial murder is that proposed by Holmes and Holmes (1994) of at least three murders with more than 30 days between the first and the last and that is the definition used throughout this book.

Notes

1. There is the possibility that prior to their marriage, Paul Bernardo and his wife Karla Homolka were also responsible for the death of Homolka's sister, but that death, if it was murder, does not fit into the pattern of the two murders with which Bernardo is charged. (The sister supposedly choked on her own vomit in front of Bernardo and Homolka while Homolka's parents were upstairs in the same house.)
2. There have been some reported cases involving the serial killing of animals. Newman and Jones (1994) recently reported the case of a person or persons mutilating and killing horses in Maryland.

3. Another theory is that the Thugs descended from a Persian tribe that settled near Delhi.
4. The term paraphilia comes from the Greek *para* meaning beyond, amiss or altered and *philia* meaning love.

References

Browning, F. and J. Gerassi. *The American Way of Crime.* New York: Putnam, 1980.

Dietz, P. Mass, serial and sensational homicides. *Bulletin of the New York Academy of Medicine* 62:477-491, 1986.

Egger, S.A. A working definition of serial murder and the reduction of linkage blindness. *Journal of Police Science and Administration* 12:348-357, 1984.

Egger, S.S. Serial murder. In S.A. Egger (ed.), *Serial Murder.* New York: Praeger, 1990.

Fernandez, E. Dead letters. *People* 40(20):111-112, 1993.

Gee, D.J. A pathologist's view of multiple murder. *Forensic Science International* 38:53-65, 1988.

Gleick E. Blood wedding. *People* 40(21):115-118, 1993.

Hazelwood, R. and J. Douglas. The lust murder. *FBI Law Enforcement Bulletin* 49(4):1-8, 1980.

Hickey, E. *Serial Killers and Their Victims.* Pacific Grove, CA: Brooks/Cole, 1991.

Holmes, R.M. and J. De Burger. Profiles in terror. *Federal Probation* 49(3):29-34, 1985.

Holmes, R.M. and J. De Burger. *Serial Murder.* Beverly Hills, CA: Sage, 1988.

Holmes R.M. and S.T. Holmes. *Murder in America.* Thousand Oaks, CA: Sage, 1994.

Lehtinen, M. The value of life. *Crime and Delinquency* 23:237-252, 1979.

Money J. Forensic sexology. *American Journal of Psychotherapy* 44:26-36, 1990.

Newman J. and R. Jones. Blood lust. *People* 41(17):187-188, 1994.

Sellin, T. *The Penalty of Death.* Beverly Hills, CA: Sage, 1980.

Sleeman, J.L. *Thug, or a Million Murders.* London: S. Low, Marston, 1933.

VICAP Alert: Charles Thurman Sinclair. *FBI Law Enforcement Bulletin* 61(2):20-21, 1992.

Chapter 3

Famous Serial Murderers

In books and articles about serial murders, the same names occur over and over again. Who are these famous serial murders and are they representative of serial murderers in general? Let us examine a few listings.

The Murderers' Who's Who

In their book, *The Murderers' Who's Who*, Gaute and Odell (1979) listed "multiple murderers" from around the world. The following is a list of people who they consider to be serial murderers:

Albert DeSalvo—U.S.
Dean Corll—U.S.
Juan Vallejo Corona—U.S.
Mary Ann Cotton—Great Britain
Martin Dumollard (and his wife)—France
Fritz Haarman (and Hans Grans)—Germany
Herman Webster Mudgett, a.k.a. H.H. Holmes—U.S.
Jack the Ripper—Great Britain
Peter Kürten—Germany
Henri Désiré Landru—France
Earle Leonard Nelson—U.S.
Carl Panzram—U.S.
Marcel Petiot—France
Heinrich Pommerencke—Germany
Charles Starkweather and Caril Ann Fugate—U.S.

Albert DeSalvo

Albert DeSalvo was never charged with murder, but he was sentenced to life imprisonment in 1967 for sex offenses and robberies. This incarceration happened before it was discovered that he had supposedly committed a series of murders and was possibly the serial killer known as the Boston Strangler. In Boston, between June 1962 and January 1964, 13 women were raped and then murdered in their homes. All of the women lived alone and ranged in age from 19 to 85. When the victims were found, their dead bodies had been propped up in obscene ways and each had a bow made from their own stockings or scarfs tied in peculiar knots around their neck.

The murders stopped after January 1964, but in November of that year, Albert DeSalvo, a 33-year-old house painter, was arrested for raping a young woman. Her description of the man led investigators to DeSalvo who was already in prison for rape. Boston police knew about DeSalvo, but they originally did not even consider him as a suspect in the Strangler investigation. He was first arrested for rape in 1962, but was paroled after serving only 11 months of a two-year sentence. He was then arrested again for a series of rapes in 1964. Judged incompetent to stand trial, he was sent to a state mental hospital where he began to boast in lurid detail to a fellow inmate how he had killed 13 women.

Born in 1931, DeSalvo came from a very poor family and his father taught him how to steal when he was five. His father was an alcoholic and extremely abusive. DeSalvo married, but he and his German-born wife, Irmgard, were not happy together. DeSalvo had a tremendous hunger for sex, and when his wife would refuse him (he claimed that he needed sex at least six times a day), he would find any woman he could and rape her. He claimed that he raped as many as 3000 women. He said it didn't matter what kind of woman he raped and killed, therefore he had no particular type of victim. His one concern, he said, was this: "It really was Woman that I wanted—not any special one, just Woman with what a woman has." Already incarcerated for life for rape, he was never tried for the Strangler crimes and wasn't even charged with them and some people believe that he was not the Boston Stangler. He claimed that he was and discussed the murders openly and in gruesome details. In November 1973, while incarcerated in the hospital section of a maximum security prison, he was murdered by another inmate (who was never identified).

Dean Arnold Corll

At the time he died, Dean Corll was a 33-year-old electrician who was employed by the Houston Power & Lighting Company. Known to his co-workers as an amicable friendly sort, but also somewhat of a loner, he was able to keep the dark side of his life a secret until he died.

Corll came from a very depressed section of Houston called The Heights where many of his young victims lived. He would lure them to his house with promises of drugs and parties. He would then make them inhale model airplane glue and when they were high enough, Corll would shackle them and then sexually torture and murder them. He was careful not to get caught: he eventually convinced two teenager acquaintances, David Brooks and later Wayne Henley, to go out and find victims for him and he also moved frequently. But in August 1973, Wayne Henley confessed to killing Corll in what he said was self-defense. He told police that for some time he had been bringing boys to Corll who would then rape, torture and murder them. Police found the bodies of 17 boys under a shed at Corll's Houston house and 10 more bodies elsewhere. Henley was tried and convicted for the murder of some of the victims and was sentenced to six 99-year prison terms.

Juan Vallejo Corona

Juan Corona, a 37-year-old Mexican laborer and contractor was charged with 25 counts of murder in California in 1971. Corona went to California in the 1950s as a migrant farm worker. He had a breakdown and was diagnosed a schizophrenic. He managed to live a quiet life with his wife and four young daughters. He was also devoutly religious and well liked by his co-workers. But in May 1971, police found the bodies of nine men buried in graves near his house. Each body had been gouged in the chest and a cross was carved in the back of each man's head. They were all positioned in the same way: face up, shirts pulled over their faces, and their arms above their heads. They were all farm workers, and some of them were migrants. Some of them seemed to have been sexually molested and they had all been killed in the previous two months. Over a period of 6 weeks, police found a total of 25 bodies of male migrant workers. In 1973, Corona was convicted on 25 counts of murder and sentenced to 25 consecutive life terms. Corona told a former Mexican consular official, "Yes, I did it, but I'm a sick man and can't be judged by the standards of other men."

Mary Ann Cotton

Mary Ann Cotton lived in Victorian England. It was discovered that she murdered her lover, her own son and her late husband's two sons by blending arsenic into their food and she was executed by hanging on March 24, 1873. However, 21 people close to her died during a period of 20 years and she is thought to have murdered at least 15 of them, probably for the insurance money or simply to free herself for the next marriage.

Martin Dumollard

In mid-nineteenth-century France, Martin Dumollard and his wife lured girls to their house on the pretext of hiring them as servants and then murdered them. In May 1861, one of the victims became suspicious on the way to the house and Dumollard tried to kill her in the street. She escaped and led the police to Dumollard. The clothing of at least 10 victims and remains of three bodies were found. Both husband and wife were found guilty of these murders in January 1862. Dumollard was guillotined and his wife was sentenced to hard labor for life.

Fritz Haarmann

Fritz Haarmann lived in the thieves' quarter of Hanover, Germany, surviving by petty theft and by informing on others to the police. He was injured in World War I, after which he seemed to suffer from epilepsy. In 1918, he began to pose as a policeman and to offer shelter to young male teenage refugees. Later joined by Hans Grans, Haarmann killed the boys and sold both their flesh (as meat) and their clothes. They killed approximately two boys a week over a 16-month period. In July 1924, Haarmann was accused of indecent behavior and a search of his lodgings revealed clothing and articles belonging to the missing boys. He was tried in 1924 and admitted killing at least 40 boys. He was found guilty and beheaded. Grans was sentenced to 12 years in prison.

Herman Webster Mudgett

Herman Mudgett (a.k.a. H.H. Holmes) moved to Chicago in 1888 to work as a chemist in a drugstore. After the owner disappeared in 1890, Mudgett was left in command. He then purchased a vacant lot across from the store and built a hotel there. Mudgett placed advertisements in newspapers offering young women lucrative work at the hotel. Over a period of three years, many, many women came to work there, and were never seen again. Mudgett would tell the women to bring everything they owned with them. Hundreds of guests also stayed at the hotel, but many of them began to disappear. During this time, Mudgett, always looking for any possible means to make a dollar, also committed insurance fraud, but he eluded the police by fleeing to Philadelphia. Surprisingly, it was the insurance scam, not the murders that brought police to investigate Mudgett's hotel.

What they found was most disturbing. The Castle, as Mudgett called his hotel, was a row of three-story buildings all joined to-gether. The ground floor was comprised of shops and the top floor housed Mudgett's own apartment and offices. In the middle, Mudgett had contructed a maze of 100 secret rooms without windows, stair-ways that went nowhere, hidden trap doors and chutes that ended in the basement which served as both torture room and mortuary. The rooms were soundproof and built so that his prisoners could not escape and doors were rigged with alarms in case they were opened. Mudgett also hooked up gas lines with which he could asphyxiate prisoners whenever the mood hit him.

Mudgett could dispose of a body by opening the chute and sending it swiftly to the cellar. Once the bodies were in the cellar, Mudgett burned them in a huge furnace or he threw them into a lime pit that was beneath a metal door on the floor. The police found instruments of torture and acid baths, as well as several female skeletons.

While Mudgett was in Philadelphia, on the run, there was a fire in his castle. Through the rubble, police found many bodies of women, men and children. Authorities said they suspected Mudgett of killing as many as 100 people. He was arrested and tried in Philadelphia, but not for his hotel murders. He confessed to 27 murders and was hanged in May 1896. He told authorities that he killed "for the pleasure of killing my fellow beings." In keeping with his request, he was buried in a casket embedded in cement that was buried under two more feet of cement because he didn't want graverobbers to have access to his body.

Jack the Ripper

"Jack the Ripper," as police and journalists dubbed him, was the mysterious murderer of five women in London in 1888. His victims were prostitutes and their bodies were horribly but skillfully mutilated with a knife—in some cases he carefully removed the internal organs of his victims. After a few months, the murders ended. There are many theories about the identity of the murderer, including known murderers of the time, an eminent doctor and even the Duke of Clarence, a member of the British Royal Family. Evidence of the placement of false clues and of a coverup involving highly placed judges and barristers has been discussed by several writers and historians.

Peter Kürten

Peter Kürten was a German factory worker who terrorized Dusseldorf in 1919. He sadistically attacked and killed children and young women, using stabbing, strangulation and bludgeoning. However, some victims survived and described their assailant. Kürten was caught by chance in May 1930, when one of his victims wrote a letter to a friend about the assault. The letter was opened by the post office after they were unable to deliver it. Kürten was charged with nine murders and guillotined in July 1931.

Henri Landru

Henri Landru was a French swindler who had been imprisoned on several occasions. During the First World War, he enticed widows by promising them marriage and then he would steal their assets and kill them. Between 1915 and 1919, he killed at least 10 such widows. Two requests to find missing widows who had disappeared with a bearded man led to a search of Landru's house and a manhunt for him. He was captured, tried and found guilty and guillotined in February 1922.

Earle Leonard Nelson

Known as the "Gorilla Murderer" because of his size and peculiar gait, Earle Leonard Nelson raped and killed 22 landladies in the United States and Canada. A childhood accident had left him brain-injured and retarded. His killing spree began in San Francisco in February 1926 and he was eventually arrested in Canada in 1927. He was found guilty and hanged in Winnipeg in January 1928.

Carl Panzram

Carl Panzram had spent much his youth in prison. He continued a life of crime as an adult, committing robberies and often killing his victims in the process. He was tried for burglary and murder in Washington, D.C. in 1928 and sentenced to 25 years in the federal penitentiary at Fort Leavenworth. Being imprisoned did not stop him; he killed the prison laundry foreman. Panzram eventually confessed to killing 21 people and was hanged in September 1930.

Marcel Petiot

Marcel Petiot was a French physician and a member of the Resistance during the Second World War. He was charged with murdering 27 people at his house in Paris. He confessed to murdering 63 people who he claimed were Nazi collaborators. Instead, Petiot appears to have made a practice of promising wealthy Jews an escape route out of France, only to kill them for their possessions. He was found guilty and guillotined in May 1946.

Heinrich Pommerencke

Heinrich Pommerencke was known as the "Beast of the Black Forest." As a teenager, he committed several rapes in Germany and Austria. Pommerencke first killed in 1959 and he murdered several more times before his capture in 1960. After confessing to 10 murders, 20 rapes and 35 assaults and burglaries, he was sentenced to 140 years in prison.

Charles Starkweather

On January 21, 1958, Charles Starkweather visited the home of his 14-year-old girlfriend, Caril Ann Fugate, shot her parents and choked her 2-year-old sister. In the next week, seven more people were shot and stabbed as the couple fled across three states. They were finally arrested in Wyoming. Starkweather was executed in the electric chair in Nebraska in June 1959 and Fugate, though sentenced to life imprisonment, was paroled in 1977. *Badlands*, an acclaimed film by the British director Terrence Malick, presents a semifictional account of the Starkweather-Fugate saga, starring Martin Sheen and Sissy Spacek.

Other Listings

In its True Crime series, Time-Life Books (1992) profiled four serial murderers in depth: Ted Bundy, who killed at least 20 young women (and possibly as many as 30) between 1973 and 1978 in Washington, Oregon, Utah, Colorado and Florida; John Wayne Gacy, who killed 33 boys and young men in Chicago between 1972 and 1978; David Berkowitz ("Son of Sam"), who killed six people and wounded seven others in New York City in 1976 and 1977; and Dennis Nilsen, who killed 15 young men in England between 1978 and 1983.[*]

Although not truly encyclopedic in treatment, Masters and Lea (1963) provide graphic details of serial murderers beginning in Roman times and covering most continents of the world, including examples of sadists, werewolves, vampires, cannibals, necrophiles and "rippers."

The Preponderance of American Serial Murderers

If one reads American books on serial murder, one gets the impression that America by far has the highest incidence of serial murderers of any nation. Of course, if foreign murders were as well-known to us, we might find that other nations have a higher incidence of serial murder. For example, Wilson and Seaman (1985) present an overview of murder from 1962 to 1982 and, because Wilson is British, the recorded incidence of serial murders is very high for Great Britain. Wilson and Seaman list 18 American serial murderers for that period—11 for Great Britain, two for West Germany and one each for Canada, India, Mexico, the Netherlands and Norway.[†]

---

[*] The book also briefly mentions Gilles de Rais (France, 1400s), "Jack the Ripper" (England, 1880s), and Peter Kürten (Germany, 1920s), as well as American serial killers Herman Mudgett (1880s), Albert Fish (1920s), Joe Ball (1930s), William Heirens (1940s), Ed Gein (1950s), Albert DeSalvo (1960s), Jerry Brudos (1960s), Juan Corona (1970s), Dean Corrll (1970s), Larry Eyler (1980s) and Richard Ramirez (1980s).

[†] The American serial murderers include: David Berkowitz ("Son of Sam"), Ted Bundy, Norman Collins, Dean Corll, Juan Corona, Albert DeSalvo, John Wayne Gacy, Edmund Kemper, Paul Knowles, Harry Lanham/Antony Knoppe, Sherman McCrary, William MacDonald, Herbert Mullin, Melvin Rees, Charles Schmid, Wayne Williams and Zodiac. The British serial murderers include: Ian Brady/Myra Hindley, Archibald Hall, "Jack the Ripper," Peter Dinsdale, Patrick MacKay, Raymond Morris, Donald Neilson, Dennis Nilsen, Peter Sutcliffe and Graham Young.

If we just consider America and Great Britain, the respective incidences of serial murderers for the 20-year period is 8.3 per 100,000
for the United States and 18.0 for Great Britain! It seems likely that
writers in each nation of the world might be able to document serial
murders in their own countries more precisely than outsiders and
hence arrive at higher incidences.

Types of Serial Murderers

Perusal of contemporary books on serial murderers gives the impression that the phenomenon is recent and that almost all are
sexually motivated. A different perspective is provided by Sifakis'
Encyclopedia of American Crime (1982). I browsed through just the As
and Bs of this large volume searching for people who fit the definition of serial murderer (i.e., at least three people killed in a period
of more than 30 days). I counted eight hit men for organized crime,
seven outlaws and gunfighters, four felons, one vigilante and six
others, only one of whom (David Berkowitz, "Son of Sam") was
recent. Few of these six "others" fit the category of serial sexual
murderer. For example, Joe Ball (1892-1938) appears to have fed
over 12 of the waitresses at his Sociable Inn in Elmendorf, Texas, to
his pet alligators for motives which remain obscure. (He committed
suicide when lawmen arrived to arrest him.) Joseph Briggen (1850-
1903) killed homeless men in California to feed his prize pigs and
Sam Brown (1828-1861) killed anyone who annoyed him, mostly in
bars in Virginia City, Nevada.

The impression given by this crime encyclopedia is that there
have always been large numbers of serial murderers in America, but
that few indeed of those identified were sexually motivated.

Comment

Any listing of serial murderers is bound to be somewhat dependent
on the particular compiler and his preferred definition of serial
murder. Should people like Adolf Hitler or his underlings and
Genghis Khan, the twelfth-century Mongol warrior, be included in
a listing of serial killers? Should the pirates and outlaws of the past
and the felons and gang members of the present be included?

Despite these issues, however, the same names do crop up again
and again in listings of serial murderers and the unbiased listings
do include many from nations other than the United States.

References

Gaute, J.H.H. and R. Odell. *The Murderers' Who's Who.* New York: Methuen, 1979.

Breitman, R. Hitler and Genghis Khan. *Journal of Contemporary History* 25:337-351, 1990.

Masters, R.E.L. and E. Lea. *Perverse Crimes in History.* New York: The Julian Press, 1963.

Serial Killers. Alexandria, VA: Time-Life Books, 1992.

Sifakis, C. *The Encyclopedia of American Crime.* New York: Facts on File, 1982.

Wilson, C. and D. Seaman. *The Encyclopedia of Modern Murder, 1962-1982.* New York: Putnam, 1985.

Chapter 4

The Frequency of Serial Murder

Modern writers on the topic of serial murder often argue that it has increased greatly in frequency in recent years and the implication is that serial murder hardly ever occurred in previous centuries or in the first part of this century.

How common is serial murder? In 1987 in the United States, there were 20,812 homicides and about 70 percent of these are cleared, that is, the murderer is identified (Lester, 1991). Holmes and De Burger (1988) suggested that about three-quarters of murders are cleared, leaving us with about 5000 unsolved murders each year. There are, of course, some murders that are never detected. Often the victims of these unsolved murders are believed to have died from natural causes, accidents or suicide. We have no idea how many of these "murders" are misclassified. In addition, there are an enormous number of persons who are listed as missing each year, especially children. Some of these people could have been murdered and their bodies never found. Given these unknowns, it is difficult to make a good estimate of the number of serial murders that occur and how many serial murderers exist in America.

Egger (1984) took the curious position that serial murderers only kill strangers. He noted that in 1982, of 21,012 criminal homicides, 3551 were known to be of strangers and in 2353, the relationship between the murderer and the victim was unknown. Thus Egger argued that the maximum number of stranger-to-stranger murders was 5904 and so the number of serial murders must be less than this.

Estimates of the number of American serial murderers have ranged from 30 to 100, but in 1988, Holmes and De Burger suggested that about 350 such murderers probably existed in the United States. They also felt that serial murder is more common today than it was in the early part of this century, with the rise in frequency becoming noticeable in the 1950s.

On the other hand, because these estimates are not based on good data, they are quite speculative. Typically, the authors of the reports are trying to arouse interest and concern in the topic of serial murder and so it is in their interest to inflate the figures (Egger, 1990). Better data, though probably underestimates, come from lists of actual serial murderers identified.

For example, Holmes and De Burger (1988) listed seven serial murderers identified in the period from 1900 to 1939 (1.75 per decade), eight from 1940 to 1959 (four each decade), five in the 1960s, 13 in the 1970s and 11 in the 1980s, though we must bear in mind that their book was published in 1988 and so does not include the full decade of the 1980s.

Holmes and Holmes (1994) updated this earlier listing and the revised figures are 28 for the period 1900 to 1939 (seven each decade), 20 from 1940 to 1959 (10 per decade), nine in the 1960s, 36 in the 1970s, 64 in the 1980s and 27 so far in the 1990s. Egger (1984) searched the *New York Times Index* from 1978 to June 1983 and found 54 serial murderers who had killed four or more people—equivalent to 98 per decade.

In contrast, Holmes and Holmes (1994) listed five *mass* murderers in the period 1940 to 1959, seven in the 1960s, 11 in the 1970s, 15 in the 1980s and 16 in the early 1990s (up until 1992). Thus, it is reasonable to state that serial (mainly sexual) murder and mass murder have increased in frequency in recent years.

Serial Murder During the 1960s

Jenkins (1992) noted that many writers spoke of a wave of serial murders beginning in the late 1960s and he undertook to explore whether this was really so. For the period 1940 to 1989, Jenkins searched for cases of serial murder, unfortunately excluding those in which political motives or financial profits were involved, thereby eliminating cases of organized and professional criminal activity. His criteria were four or more murders in a period greater than 72 hours. He used three major newspapers (the *New York Times, Los Angeles Times* and *Chicago Tribune*), secondary sources on serial murder and a recent encyclopedia of serial murder (Newton, 1990). The possibility that the trend toward chain ownership of newspapers during the period studied affected newspaper reporting of serial murder was presumed to have little effect on the results since

Jenkins also used secondary sources and the recent encyclopedia. The possibility that police agencies were more willing to explore whether a particular suspect might have been a serial murderer later in the period was thought to be unlikely.

For the period 1940 to 1964, Jenkins identified 30 cases of serial murder, seven of which were extreme (that is, with eight or more victims). Eleven were lust murders, nine were irrational or berserk murders, five were property crimes, four were poisonings partly for financial gain while one case defied classification. The transition years from 1965 to 1969 witnessed 19 cases of serial murder, one every 96 days.

Between 1970 and 1990, there were 187 cases of serial murder, of which 94 were extreme. Thus, the increase was from one serial murder every 10 months (and an extreme case every 43 months) to one case every 39 days (and an extreme case every 77 days), an eightfold increase for all cases and a sixteenfold increase for extreme cases. Extreme cases are important since these are much more likely to have been reported and, therefore, identified in Jenkins' study. Jenkins concluded that the increase in serial murder was a genuine phenomenon.

How might this increase be explained? Jenkins focused on the transitional period 1965 to 1969. He first noted social factors.

1. America experienced changes in demographic composition, with an increased proportion of people in their teens and twenties, which itself has been shown to be related to an increase in overall violence. However, the increase in the general homicide rate rose from 4.7 per 100,000 per year in 1960 to only 8.3 in 1970 and peaked at 10.7 in 1980. Thus, the increase was only twofold, not eightfold as with was serial murder.

2. The baby boomer generation may have promoted aggressive behavior with sexual motivation because drugs were widely available and heavily consumed—especially hallucinogens— during the later 1960s (which may have disinhibited some of those who used them), as was sexually stimulating imagery arising from the "hippie" subculture.

3. There may also have been an increase in the pool of possible victims, since increased sexual freedom, geographical mobility and acceptance of deviancy may have made it easier for potential murderers to have easier access to possible victims,

whose disappearance may have been less immediately noticed.

4. At the same time, there was a move to deinstitutionalize American psychiatric patients, so that the resident population in mental health facilities fell from more than half a million in 1955 to less than a quarter of a million in 1975. Deinstitutionalization occurred after a steady growth in the inpatient population until 1955. Also, the criminal justice system witnessed a shortening of sentences and actual time served, an emphasis on outpatient community care facilities and attacks on the "sexual psychopath" laws that had been used to imprison sexual offenders for long periods of time. Thus, more people who were at risk for murdering were sent back into society in the late 1960s and thereafter. Indeed, some of those who committed serial murders after 1965 had previously been in psychiatric institutions and prisons for brief periods of time for acts of violence and, in retrospect, were clearly released prematurely. Richard Chase, the "Vampire of Sacramento" who terrorized Californians in the 1970s, was obviously psychotic and would probably have been institutionalized in the 1940s. Some serial murderers themselves even tried to warn authorities of their potential for violence, but to no avail. Carroll Cole, for example, warned doctors at the institutions in which he was placed of his sadistic and violent impulses toward women, but he was discharged anyway, only to kill 13 people beginning in 1970.

Jenkins concluded, therefore, that the increase in (primarily sexual) serial murder in the 1960s was a real phenomenon (supporting an "objectivist" view), rather than a reflection of fashions in attention and reporting (a "constructionist" view) and merited a search for the social conditions that may have caused the murder wave of the 1970s.

Is Serial Murder a Modern Phenomenon?

It is commonly held that serial murder is a modern phenomenon. A perusal of historical records indicates that this is not true. Hickey (1991) gave several historical examples. In the early 1400s in Scotland, for example, Sawney Beane and his family took up residence in a cave on the beach and murdered travelers for their money. To avoid detection, they killed every victim and they often ate parts of the bodies because they were hungry. They disposed of limbs by throwing them into the sea and occasionally these parts washed ashore. Beane had 12 children and 32 grandchildren during this time, most the result of incest. When the family was finally discovered and arrested, the authorities found boxes of jewels and other valuables, parts of human bodies hung up to dry and other parts that had been pickled. The Beanes were executed without trial (Kerman, 1962).

Another example, also from the 1400s, is Gilles de Rais. He fought along with Joan of Arc in France, but after her defeat and death he became mentally imbalanced and murdered and mutilated a young boy. Discovering that he enjoyed this, he began to kill boys en masse, perhaps several hundred in all, drinking their blood and having sexual intercourse with their dead bodies (Hickey, 1991).

Record-keeping was highly unreliable in times past and crime detection was very rudimentary (the authorities would have had great difficulty in identifying a serial murderer's work) and so the true incidence of serial murder in premodern times is unknown. Jenkins (1989) noted that in 1890 there were only 15 officers on the Philadelphia detective force. Furthermore, accuracy in certifying the mode of death was not considered overly important. In Philadelphia, almost all the bodies found in the rivers were described as victims of drowning (Lane, 1979). It is fair to say, however, that serial murderers have undoubtedly always existed.

Jenkins (1989) searched for examples of serial murder in the United States from 1900 to 1940. He noted that other writers were able to locate only a few serial murderers. For example, Leyton (1986) mentioned only six cases between 1921 and 1950 compared to 41 from 1971 to 1985. Jenkins searched the *New York Times* and found 24 instances of serial murders in which the number of victims was 10 or more in the period from 1900 to 1940. In the early part of this century, Chicago had the reputation of being the serial murder "capital" of the country, much as California is today. Jenkins estimated that there were probably 80 or more serial murderers with five or more victims in this period—this despite the fact that racial biases were clear in law enforcement response to crime. For example, Albert Fish, who murdered and cannibalized children between 1910 and 1935, deliberately preyed on black children in New York and Washington, D.C. because he knew that the authorities were mainly concerned about missing whites. Leo Frank was lynched after allegedly killing a white girl in Atlanta in 1915, although the earlier murders of 20 black women in the city had aroused little public concern.

In the early part of this century, the victims of serial murderers were often poor and newly arrived immigrants, the kinds of people whose disappearance was of little concern to the community. Even today, the victims of serial murderers are often the powerless and rootless, such as children, prostitutes or vagrants.

It must be remembered that the population of the United States was much smaller in the first part of this century—about 120 million in 1920. Therefore, the rate of extreme serial murders per year for the period 1900 to 1940 is 0.5 per 100,000 per year. Although Holmes and Holmes (1994) reported 64 serial murderers in the U.S. during the 1980s, they do not list the number of victims for each case and so we cannot calculate a comparable rate of extreme serial murder.

More importantly, Brown (1991) has noted that the sexually motivated serial killer of modern times was known in the past, but under different labels. If one searches for instances of lust murder, necrophilia (committing sexual acts with corpses) and vampirism (including necrosadism and necrophagia),* many cases can be found in past centuries. Going further back, cases of sexual serial murder become mixed up with tales of vampires and werewolves. Indeed, cases of necrophilia can be found as far back as ancient Egypt, where families kept the bodies of deceased female members for several days to prevent sexual abuse of the corpse by the embalmers.

Finally, we should note that interest in serial murderers has always existed and books of cases have been found from earlier times. For example, Bolitho (1926) presented five cases of serial murderers from Great Britain, France and Germany, including Burke and Hare, who murdered people in order to sell their bodies to physicians for dissection and study, and Logan (1928) presented the cases of 19 infamous multiple murderers.

Jenkins (1989) noted that the two modern countries with the highest frequency of serial murder are the United States and Germany. Although the precise reasons for the high rate of serial murder in these two countries are unclear, Jenkins speculates that perhaps it is a result in part of the large transient populations that are a feature of both the U.S. and postwar Germany.

---

* In previous centuries, vampirism referred to murder, with or without rape, associated with eating parts of the body. In the twentieth century, vampirism has been more closely associated with consuming the blood of a victim who has been raped and usually murdered.

Jenkins (1988) searched for records of serial murders in England and Wales from 1940 to 1985, using a criterion of at least four victims and excluding political and professional killers. He identified 12 cases, accounting for 107 victims over the 46-year period, or about 1.7 percent of all murder victims.

The Changing Character of the Serial Killer

Leyton (1986) has argued that the profile of the serial killer has changed over the centuries. The preindustrial serial killer was an aristocrat who preyed on his peasants; the early industrial-era serial killer was a newly established bourgeois who killed prostitutes, homeless boys and housemaids; the modern serial killer is a failed bourgeois who stalks university women and other middle-class victims.

In preindustrial times, the aristocracy was under attack by the peasant and merchant classes. Peasant revolts were common in Europe in the thirteenth, fourteenth and fifteenth centuries and the established order sought to reimpose its authority through savage repression. It is in this context that a nobleman like Baron Gilles de Rais (1404-1440) murdered several hundred young boys.

Toward the end of the eighteenth century, the rising middle classes were greatly concerned with disciplining the lower classes who threatened their newly won position. The majority of the serial killers of this era were middle-class functionaries (teachers, doctors and civil servants) who killed members of the lower classes, such as prostitutes and housemaids, acting as self-appointed enforcers of the new moral order. Dr. Thomas Cream, for example, poisoned prostitutes in London in the 1890s. However, a minority of the killers were lower-class outcasts, full of rage against their exclusion from the new social order, killers such as Carl Panzram in America in the early 1900s.

Finally, Leyton (1986) noted that modern serial killers are often ambitious but untalented middle-class individuals who have found it difficult to achieve any measure of success. In a culture that stresses competitive individualism and material prosperity (Lasch, 1979) and the severing of ties of responsibility between people (Ehrenreich, 1983), they react to the frustration of their blocked social mobility by transforming their fantasies of revenge into reality. They come from the working and lower middle classes, from the ranks of security guards, computer operators and postal clerks. They often target middle-class victims on college campuses or in shopping malls. Some are conscious of this choice, such as Mark Essex and

Ted Bundy, while others seem not to be, such as Albert DeSalvo. On the surface, they appear to be killing for sexual pleasure, but there is also a burning grudge resulting from their failed ambition.

Wilson (1985) has made a similar point—that the character type of the serial murderer has changed over the years. The motiveless and sadistic violence committed by social failures that we witness today was once the sport of tyrants or men of wealth. But Wilson feels that even in the past such crimes were rare. He speculates that the modern phenomenon is a result of increased stress and a growing resentment against society by people of average or above-average intelligence who feel that society restricts their ability to use of their talents. People now search for someone or something to blame for their failures (and perhaps their unhappiness) and they turn to "magical thinking" to ease their distress. Magical thinking is an illogical attempt to avoid the effort of exerting self-control and to obtain instant happiness and freedom from pain. For example, Charles Manson resented the bourgeoisie who he believed were denying him the success he felt he deserved. The "motive" behind the murders that Manson and his followers committed was to start a race war between blacks and whites. However, Manson might just as well have stoned cats, according to Wilson, to express his resentment since his actual choice of victims made no apparent sense.

Wilson (1985) and Jackson (1994) have both suggested that the motives of serial killers have changed and they used the hierarchy of needs proposed by Abraham Maslow (1970) to illustrate this. Maslow proposed five levels of human needs: physiological needs (such as for air and food); safety and security needs; the need to belong (social relationships with others, to be loved and to love and to belong to a culture); esteem needs (to feel good about yourself and to have others value you) and self-actualization needs (to realize your potential). Wilson and Jackson suggested that serial murderers in the 1700s and 1800s killed because they were poor and hungry, that is, to satisfy physiological needs. Later they killed for domestic security such as a home and still later for love and sex. Today, esteem needs play a larger role—the desire for attention and respect.

The Cost of Serial Murder

The cost to society from serial murder is great. There are costs incurred simply through the loss of life—the loss of productive years from the victims. There are the costs of the suffering of the victim's friends and relatives who have more difficulty coping with this type of horrific loss than they would from a death due to natural causes. There are costs to society by the fear that such murders generate. And finally there are costs incurred in tracking down serial killers, conducting trials, keeping them imprisoned for long periods of time and/or executing them. For example, when the police suspect a serial killer is at work, large numbers of officers and resources are mobilized in order to find and capture the murderer. Holmes and De Burger estimated that the overall effort to catch Washington state's "Green River Killer," who was responsible for 32 murders in the 1980s, employed 46 full-time police officers, who investigated some 200 suspects, and generated 2000 pages of paperwork daily at a cost of $2 million a year.

References

Bolitho, W. *Murder for Profit.* Garden City, NY: Garden City Publishing Company, 1926.

Brown, J.S. The historical similarity of 20th century serial sexual homicide to pre-20th century occurrences of vampirism. *American Journal of Forensic Psychiatry* 12(2):11-24, 1991.

Egger, S.A. A working definition of serial murder and the reduction of linkage blindness. *Journal of Police Science and Administration* 12:348-357, 1984.

Egger, S.A. Serial murder. In S.A. Egger (ed.), *Serial Murder.* New York: Praeger, 1990.

Ehrenreich, B. *The Hearts of Men.* New York: Anchor, 1983.

Hickey, E.W. *Serial Murderers and Their Victims.* Pacific Grove, CA: Brooks/Cole, 1991.

Holmes, R.M. and J. De Burger. *Serial Murder.* Beverly Hills, CA: Sage, 1988.

Holmes, R.M. and S.T. Holmes. *Murder in America.* Thousand Oaks, CA: Sage, 1994.

Jackson, D. Serial killers and the people who love them. *Village Voice* 39 (12, March 22):26-32, 1994.

Jenkins, P. Serial murder in England, 1940-1985. *Journal of Criminal Justice* 16:1-15, 1988.

Jenkins, P. Serial murder in the United States, 1900-1940. *Journal of Criminal Justice* 17:377-397, 1989.

Jenkins, P. A murder "wave"? *Criminal Justice Review* 17(1): 1-19, 1992.

Kerman, S.L. *The Newgate Calendar.* New York: Capricorn, 1962.

Lane, R. *Violent Death in the City.* Cambridge, MA: Harvard University Press, 1979.

Lasch, C. *The Culture of Narcissism.* New York: Warner, 1979.

Lester, D. *Questions and Answers About Murder.* Philadelphia: The Charles Press, 1991.

Leyton, E. *Compulsive Killers.* New York: New York University Press, 1986.

Logan, G.B.H. *Masters of Crime.* London: Stanley Paul, 1928.

Maslow, A.H. *Motivation and Personality.* New York: Harper and Row, 1970.

Newton, M. *Hunting Humans.* Port Townsend, WA: Loompanics, 1990.

Wilson C. The age of murder. In C. Wilson and D. Seaman (eds.), *The Encyclopedia of Modern Murder, 1962-1982.* New York: Putnam, 1985.

Chapter 5

Public Concern

There has been a tremendous growth in the general public's concern over the "problem" of serial murder. That individuals can commit murder again and again without being caught arouses great anxiety. This is particularly true for the cases that receive the most attention—murders that involve sexually sadistic acts. Several scholars have examined why this anxiety is greatly stimulated in some eras and less so in others.

Sensational Homicides

Dietz (1986) noted that the public's concern about serial murder (and murder in general) is shaped to some extent by what they read about murder in the press. From a perusal of tabloids, Dietz noted informally that in America, five types of murders receive a share of attention that is disproportionate to their frequency: sexually sadistic murders with sexual assault, torture and mutilation of the victim; homicides followed by post-death injuries such as decapitation or cannibalism; homicide with elements of satanism or some other cult activity; homicides in which the murderer or victim is a celebrity; and murder within the nuclear family (such as infanticide, matricide or patricide).

In an analysis of articles in detective magazines (such as *Detective World* and *True Detective*), Dietz and his associates (1986) found that 38 percent of the homicides involved torture of the victim. Female victims were almost always sexually assaulted prior to their murder, whereas only about 2 percent of all homicides occur in the context of sexual assault. Mutilation themes often appeared on the covers of these magazines, with titles such as "Mutilations on Mulberry Street," and vampire and cannibal themes were frequent, with titles such as "The Holy Vampire Drank His Victim's Blood." Cult and satanic rituals were also common themes, with titles such as "Satanist Smiled as He Snuffed the Snitch."

Can Magazines Cause Serial Murder?

The study of detective magazines raises the question of whether such material can contribute to the cause of murder, sexual assault and serial murder. Dietz (1986) presented several cases of sexual sadists who liked detective magazines. One patient, who had started his sexual involvement with relatives and acquaintances at the age of 10, liked to masturbate while looking at the covers and contents of detective magazines because they came closest to matching his sexual fantasies, although he claimed never to have acted these out.

Dietz and his colleagues described one serial killer with a fondness for detective magazines, a 35-year-old married white male who was charged with committing more than 10 murders. He regarded masturbation as shameful and dirty and, though familiar with explicitly sexual magazines, had never been to an adult bookstore or X-rated movie. He considered the films *The Exorcist* and *Psycho* as influential in his life and he confessed to liking the covers of detective magazines.

After an adolescence marked by criminal acts such as vandalism and burglary, the man married and divorced several times. The divorces occurred primarily because he violently beat his wives. While in prison for armed robbery, he carried on a sexual relationship with his 7-year-old daughter (begun during a conjugal visit to the prison). After his release, he lived with his daughter as husband and wife until she escaped to her grandparents. He then found a new lover (who became his sixth wife) and together they began a two-year series of rapes and murders. His wife helped him procure young girls who he would then beat, torture, rape and kill. Then his wife would help him conceal the evidence. He killed the victims mainly to prevent them from talking rather than for pleasure.

The man had never known his father who had been executed for murdering both a policeman and a correctional officer. After he found out about his father's life, he came to believe that his father "lived within him." His mother had been married four times and had many extramarital affairs. She told her son that she had been raped by his father when she was only nine.

The man was a bed-wetter until the age of 13 and his mother beat him for this and subjected him to ridicule in public. One of his stepfathers not only beat him "relentlessly," but also burned him and made him drink his own urine. He was knocked unconscious on several occasions and was comatose briefly at the age of 16 and then for a week when he was 20.

Neuropsychological testing suggested damage to the right frontal lobe of his brain and the subject was diagnosed as having had a psychotic breakdown with paranoid delusions and suicidal ideation in his twenties after the death of his brother.

Dietz commented that the detective magazines obviously did not cause this man's sexually sadistic and murderous behavior. However, Dietz noted that such magazines could motivate a latent sadist to commit crimes (particularly if he uses them to facilitate masturbation), by adding imagery to his sexual fantasies and by lessening the extent to which he believes that his desires are socially unacceptable. In other words, the magazines may provide validation for the acceptability of his desires. Criminals may also think that their crimes may bring them publicity and attention; the potential murderer may imagine his own story described in lurid detail in a future issue of the magazine. These magazines are also a source of information for techniques on committing crimes, on the errors made by previous offenders and on the methods used by law enforcement agencies to track down criminals. Dietz located both criminals and law enforcement officers who used these magazines as a source of continuing education. Finally, the advertisements in the detective magazines provide access to weapons and information and paraphernalia useful for committing crimes, including how to obtain false law enforcement identification.

In a later study, Stack (1989) found that publicity about serial and mass murders on major television networks during the period of 1968 to 1980 did not have any impact on the general monthly murder rate in America. However, there was a tendency for publicized gangland murders to be associated with an increase in monthly suicide rates.

Glorification of the Serial Killer

The general public is undeniably fascinated by serial killers, as the myriad of TV shows, films and stories about them attest. There is also, as Caputi (1987, 1990) pointed out, a tendency to glorify the serial killer. She noted, for example, that in 1988, Great Britain celebrated the centennial of the Jack the Ripper murders with T-shirts, buttons, mugs, computer games and a blood-red cocktail in bars (Cameron, 1988). In 1977, after Ted Bundy escaped from a

Colorado prison, a folk singer in Aspen sang, "So let's salute the mighty Bundy, here on Friday, gone on Monday...It's hard to keep a good man down" (Winn and Merrill, 1980, p. 217). *Time* (1994) noted that John Wayne Gacy had a 900 telephone number offering recorded messages—$23.88 for a 12-minute call. Charles Manson had a line of caps, surfer pants and T-shirts produced, and had a special typeface named after him (until protests made the typographers change the name of the font to Mason). Zoglin (1994) documented the spate of interviews with serial murderers on prime-time television shows, including *Turning Point* (ABC), *Dateline* (NBC) and *48 Hours* (CBS). As well, any information about serial killers—especially their executions—is always headline material on television and in the newspaper.

Caputi argues convincingly that the glorification of serial killers stems from the supremacy of males in patriarchal societies. Rather than seeing serial killers who torture and kill women as insane monsters, she views them as logical, if extreme, products of a misogynist culture, a view shared by Cameron and Frazer (1987). She also raises the possibility that the media, by giving such killers tremendous publicity, may prolong their killing sprees (as David Berkowitz, the "Son of Sam" killer, acknowledged himself in 1977) and may also offer the suggestion that people experiment with this activity.

Jackson (1994) presented case examples of everyday people who were fascinated, even obsessed, by serial killers. For example, a funeral director named Randall Phillip from Baton Rouge, Louisiana visited serial killers in prison, such as Wayne Henley, a third partner in the partner-serial killings of Dean Corll and David Brooks who killed 27 young men (see Chapter 3). Phillip, described by Jackson as the founder of a magazine about serial killers called *Fuck*, acted as an agent for John Wayne Gacy to sell his artwork. He collects memorabilia of serial killers in a room that he keeps sealed off from his wife and son. According to Jackson, celebrities like David Letterman and Johnny Depp buy and collect the artwork of serial killers as a hobby.

This fascination with serial killers is sometimes encouraged by the killers themselves. John Wayne Gacy wrote to over 23,000 people, most of whom wrote to him first, in the last 12 years of his life and he funded his letter writing by selling his artwork. The intrigue is further fueled by the media. For example, television shows *(The Commish)* and comic books *(Psycho Killers)* frequently use serial and other types of murder as a plot. *Unsolved Mysteries,* as the name implies, concentrates on crimes that have never been solved. This show is a big hit and viewers call an 800 number with any tips they may be able to offer the police. In fact, the information offered on the show together with viewer tips has solved a good number of cases. People are fascinated with the cop shows such as *Top Cops* and *Highway Patrol* that cover true stories with real footage and carefully arranged dramatizations. These television shows are aired during prime time, and for an obvious reason; people are fascinated with crime. When art galleries display the artwork of serial killers they receive big crowds and apparently there are even serial killer trading cards. The lyrics to several rock songs are about killers and this often serves to romanticize the subject. The Rolling Stone's "Midnight Rambler" is about Jack the Ripper and "I Don't Like Mondays" (by the Boomtown Rats), is the true story about a girl who several years ago walked into her classroom one day and shot all of her classmates; when asked why she had done it, she replied, "I don't like Mondays." Also, *Guns N' Roses* did a remake of a song that Charles Manson wrote, in a way perhaps showing some kind of tribute to the killer. *20/20, Dateline* and other prime-time television newsmagazines often do shows on murderers and sometimes offer an 800 number for information from viewers. Robert Ressler, an ex-FBI agent whose scholarly work is reviewed in this book, frequently gets telephone calls from shows such as *Geraldo* and *Hard Copy*, asking him to line up interviews with serial killers, as if he were a serial killer booking agent. Jackson hypothesizes that most persons who are fascinated by serial killers are loners, but magazines and computer networks are beginning to enable these loners to link up and socialize with one another. Jackson describes one case in some detail. A Los Angeles man and his wife publish a slick underground magazine that deals with violence and hate. They have a poster on the wall of their apartment that shows a teenage boy with his face shot off. They collect video tapes that feature sadism and self-mutilation, acts that are often combined with sex. The man gave Jackson an autobiographical account of his life and it resembles the life stories of more than a few serial killers. He was an unplanned and unwanted child. The man's father was an alcoholic and beat his wife and children. His brother was murdered in Paris and he himself has assault records in three states. He told Jackson, "There's a part where I can relate to what [serial killers] went through.... The rage they must've felt to get to that point. The frustration.... This society isn't all good, it's mostly bad" (p. 29). He respects anyone, he claims, who goes against social mandates and he acts out his feelings in a most flagrant and destructive way. His rage makes him want everyone elses life to be as horrible as his own. Jackson feels that this man is so overinvolved with his own pain, anger and misery-laden upbringing that the experiences of others and the effects he may have on them, no matter how bad, are irrelevant to him. The man's identity is based entirely on his horrible life and this fuels his anger and resentment.

The Serial Killer in Film

Blennerhassett (1993) has traced the development of film portrayal of the serial killer which has become one of the most frightening images of our time. Robert Louis Stevenson's *Dr. Jekyll and Mr. Hyde* was one of the first crime stories to be made into a film and its theme, though technically the psychiatric diagnosis of a multiple personality, is really about a person who is overcome by his own repressed pathological tendencies. In the theory of personality proposed by Carl Jung (Progroff, 1973), this facet of our mind is represented by a complex called the "shadow." The shadow is a subpersonality (one component of our total personality) that contains our feelings of inferiority and our unacceptable wishes and stands in opposition to our "persona" which is the socially acceptable subpersonality we present to others in our everyday social interactions. Dr. Jekyll cannot assimilate his shadow, but rather is possessed by it.

Alfred Hitchcock's film *Psycho* became the next standard by which such films were judged, with links between sexuality and violence, voyeurism and sadism, and misogyny and gender confusion. More recently, the "slasher" films, such as the *Halloween,* and the *Friday the 13th* and *Elm Street* series, feature savage characters who brutally kill again and again. These films still enjoy enormous popularity among moviegoers and they are shown constantly on television. The movie *The Silence of the Lambs* (1993) appeals to more sophisticated audiences because the serial killer is intellectually gifted.

Blennerhassett noted that this mythic figure of the twentieth century has parallels in earlier times. Sexual violence was an important element of the vampire and werewolf myths of the eighteenth and nineteenth centuries (Bourguignon, 1983) and, we might add, in the Harlequin myths of earlier centuries (McClelland, 1963) in which Harlequin is both a lover and a killer who carries Columbine off to the underworld.

Thus, Blennerhassett implies that we need stories that have characters embodying the shadow, that aspect of our personality containing our forbidden impulses and that the serial killer satisfies this need in modern times. After all, is this not the traditional struggle between good and evil, which in earlier times was cast as the struggle between God and the Devil? Whereas our ancestors were terrified by images of Satan, we imagine ourselves to be more sophisticated and need a human embodiment of evil to terrify us.

A Case Study of Public Concern: England

Jenkins (1991) noted that during the 1980s, serial murder came to be viewed in England as a new and frightening social menace. In 1986, for example, there was a flood of media reports about a "wave" of such cases. Jenkins examined whether in fact there was a "wave" of serial murder in England at that time and he then examined the factors leading to the growth of concern.

British records are quite comprehensive and Jenkins was able to locate all cases of serial murder (with four or more victims) occurring between 1880 and 1990 in England and Wales over a period greater than 72 hours. He found 25 cases, only five of which had 10 or more victims. This compares to almost 700 cases in America, Jenkins claimed, of which about 100 had 10 or more victims.

Jenkins noted that the 1980s saw the same number of serial murders in England and Wales as did the 1940s or the 1960s. Thus, unlike America, there has been no apparent increase in the frequency of serial murder during this period of heightened public concern.

Jenkins argued that public attitudes were shaped by several important cases of serial murder. Peter Sutcliffe, the "Yorkshire Ripper," killed 13 women in northern English towns during the 1970s, arousing a public concern unparalleled since Jack the Ripper in the 1880s. The Yorkshire Ripper was used to popularize feminist theories about rape and serial murder as part of a pattern of indiscriminate violence by men against women. In 1986, four serial murderers aroused public concern anew and there was a shift from viewing such murderers as disturbed individuals to seeing them as a social phenomenon. The problem, it was alleged, lay in society rather than in the individual. Conservatives used the cases to urge action against pornography, child exploitation and even homosexuality.

One of the cases in 1986 involved child victims and this became a major focus of concern. Though child murder showed no general increase during the 1980s in England, the police began to show great interest in child victims and Jenkins suggested that this was because the English police wanted closer coordination between the different police forces and the social service agencies. This integration had been resisted by left-wing politicians and civil libertarians, as well as some police administrators, who felt that coordination would result in loss of civil liberties for the general public and loss of autonomy for local police departments.

Thus, Jenkins argued that the serial murders in England in the 1980s served as a social trauma that particular political groups could use in arguing for their particular political positions and their preferred social programs.

Public Concern: The American Panic of 1983-85

Jenkins (1988) turned his attention to America, noting that media scares are common, whether over drug abuse invading cities and suburbs, or widespread sexual permissiveness, or the abduction of teenagers. Some of the panics tap into long-standing xenophobia and anti-immigrant biases, while others seem to serve bureaucratic and governmental purposes. The 1980s in America witnessed panic over crack cocaine, child sexual abuse, satanism, sex and violence in rock lyrics, AIDS and, especially in the period from 1983 to 1985, serial murder.

In the mid-1980s, the American media began to focus on a virtual epidemic of serial murder involving an unprecedented incidence of sexual assault and mutilation, with reports of as many as 300 serial murderers roaming the nation, accounting for some 4000 victims each year. Jenkins noted that many writers, including scholars, misinterpreted the crime statistics. Many murders seem motiveless, at least at the time they are entered in federal crime reports. Many involve strangers and some remain unsolved. There is no logical reason to assign all of these "motiveless," stranger-to-stranger and unsolved murders to serial murderers. Since local police departments rarely correct their initial reports to match those of the federal authorities, there is no reason to trust the accuracy of government data on motives and clearance rates. Many of the murders by strangers of strangers in the 1980s were the result of drug deals gone awry. Jenkins noted that recent reasonable estimates settled on a national total of about 35 serial murderers accounting for perhaps 200 victims a year, no more than 2 or 3 percent of the total murders committed in any given year in America.

Although the number of confirmed serial murderers did not increase in this period as compared to the previous five or 10 years, the panic seemed to have started in the fall of 1983 when Henry Lee

Lucas confessed to the murder of as many as 300 people, including several children. (By the end of 1985, it was concluded that the actual number of his victims was closer to 10.)

Jenkins noted that the panic over serial murder furnished support for the FBI to set up a center for the study of violent crime at their academy in Quantico, Virginia, together with a centralized violent criminal apprehension program that had been opposed by civil libertarians and local law enforcement agencies. The new focus on serial murder also reflected a shift in attitudes toward crime and criminals in America. The violent criminal was now seen as the embodiment of evil and many conservatives welcomed this stereotype. In this new atmosphere, criminals were no longer the victims of social wrongs and crime could no longer be remedied simply by changing the society. Instead, criminals were cast in the role of pathological predators upon society. Thus, capital punishment for murderers and long prison terms for other criminals became more popular with mainstream Americans. Jenkins does not suggest that the media was motivated by criminal justice aims or conservative political views. However, the media is famous for relying on "experts" to obtain information and quotes for their articles and broadcasts, and these sources are famous for interpreting facts and events to suit their own purposes.

References

Blennerhassett, R. The serial killer in film. *Irish Journal of Psychological Medicine* 10:101-104, 1993.

Bourguignon, A. Vampirism and autovampirism. In L.B. Schlesinger and E. Revich (eds.), *Sexual Dynamics of Antisocial Behavior.* Springfield, IL: Charles C Thomas, 1983.

Cameron, D. That's entertainment? *Trouble and Strife* 13:17-19, 1988.

Cameron, D. and E. Frazer. *The Lust to Kill.* New York: New York University Press, 1987.

Caputi, J. *The Age of Sex Crime.* Bowling Green, OH: Bowling Green University Press, 1987.

Caputi, J. The new Founding Fathers. *Journal of American Culture* 13(3):1-12, 1990.

Dietz, P.E. Mass, serial and sensational homicides. *Bulletin of the New York Academy of Medicine* 62:477-491, 1986.

Dietz, P.E., B. Harry and R.R. Hazelwood. Detective magazines. *Journal of Forensic Sciences* 31:197-211, 1986.

Jackson, D. Serial killers and the people who love them. *Village Voice* 39(12, March 22):26-32, 1994.

Jenkins, P. Myth and murder. *Criminal Justice Research Bulletin* 3(11):1-7, 1988.

Jenkins, P. Changing perceptions of serial murder in contemporary England. *Journal of Contemporary Criminal Justice* 7:210-231, 1991.

McClelland, D. The Harlequin complex. In J.W. White (ed.), *The Study of Lives.* New York: Atherton, 1963.

Progroff, I. *Jung's Psychology and Its Social Meaning.* Garden City, NY: Anchor, 1973.

Serial chic. *Time* 143(12, March 21):23, 1994.

Stack, S. The effect of publicized mass murders and murder-suicides on lethal violence, 1968-1980. *Social Psychiatry and Psychiatric Epidemiology* 24:202-208, 1989.

Winn, S. and D. Merrill. *Ted Bundy.* New York: Bantam, 1980.

Zoglin, R. Manson family values. *Time* 143(12, March 21):77, 1994.

Chapter 6

Characteristics of Serial Murderers

It is easy to read the cases of one or two particular serial murderers and decide that there is a common characteristic or pattern in their makeup. The difficult task is to show that this characteristic is indeed common to many, if not most, serial murderers. For example, I recently received a letter pointing out that "a highly disproportionate percentage of [American] mass murderers and serial killers come from the homosexual community." The writer's evidence consisted of four serial killers: Jeffrey Dahmer, John Wayne Gacy, Henry Lee Lucas and Charles Manson. This kind of conclusion, based on only four cases, is not convincing and does not offer any reliable data.

Many writers on the topic have made conflicting observations. For example, some writers feel that psychotic serial murderers are different from those who are sexually motivated; others object to this distinction. Brown (1991a) argued that psychotic serial murderers may have a sexual motivation and that some sexual serial murderers may be psychotic.

This anecdotal and armchair speculation is simply unacceptable, certainly not for any study that is meaningful. In order to arrive at a reliable portrait of the serial murderer, it is necessary to obtain from a large sample of subjects an accurate count of the frequency of characteristics and the same count must be done on a comparison group, for example, single-victim killers or armed robbers, or even the general population, perhaps also matched for gender and age. Unfortunately, this has not yet been done. Although some studies have counted the frequency of certain characteristics in serial murderers, few studies have compared a sample of serial murderers with a sample of mass or one-time murderers.

48

Studies of Samples of Serial Killers

Dickson

Dickson (1958) examined the cases of 14 famous serial murderers from around the world. He noted that the motives of serial murderers are not as varied as those of one-time murderers. He identified profit and perversion as his subjects' two main motives. Dickson found that a common trait of serial murderers motivated by perversion was that they usually came from a dysfunctional family and that they had had a traumatic childhood. Those who murdered for profit were relatively well-educated, unlike those who killed for perverted reasons, and both types of serial murderers felt physically inferior to other people. Many of the serial murderers had engaged in theft or fraud prior to committing murder and many had been imprisoned for these kinds of crimes. This type of background is rarely found in one-time murderers. Poverty and a military service record were not common in serial murderers who killed for motives of profit or for perverted reasons.

From the serial murderers he studied, Dickson described the typical serial murderer in the following way: a small, well-dressed, sociable and charming man in his forties, who neither smokes, drinks nor is inclined to swear and is often a practicing Christian. His military history, if any, was unheroic. If he is a murderer of the perverted type, his school-days were unpleasant and if he murders for profit, he was more successful at school. He does not talk much about his experiences during his twenties because he was often imprisoned during that time. He is reticent about his domestic life and is either separated or divorced from his wife or, if unmarried, has a female friend who is kept in the background. He does not have much of a sense of humor and is rather tight-fisted with his money. His conversation centers on the present and he likes to discuss the business acumen that he thinks he possesses.

Lunde

Lunde (1979) studied a sample of 40 mass and serial murderers and concluded that almost all of them were "insane." He concluded also that American mass and serial murderers are almost always white males and, unlike one-time murderers, are rarely heavy users of alcohol or drugs. Whereas the one-time murderer most often murders a close relative or friend (although during an armed robbery, for example, he may kill a complete stranger), mass and serial murderers more often target people with particular attributes that have special significance for them. The victims are unaware of their special significance.

Lunde argued that most mass and serial murderers are either schizophrenics (especially of the paranoid type) or sexual sadists. The sexual sadist shows very little evidence of psychotic symptoms, but has associated sexuality with violence, often from an early age. Thus, signs of sexual deviation and violence appear early in his life, with behaviors such as deviant masturbation fantasies and cruelty to animals. Sexual sadists are sometimes found to have a minor criminal record involving burglaries. Lunde's study is flawed by his failure to distinguish the serial killers from the mass murderers and to study the two groups separately.

Levin and Fox

Levin and Fox (1985) identified 42 serial and mass murderers from newspaper reports from 1974 to 1979 and then collected a second sample of 137 offenders from FBI files. The typical offender was a white male in his twenties or thirties. The serial murderers usually strangled or beat their victims and their principal motives were money, expediency, jealousy or lust. Almost 18 percent of the serial and mass murders in the Levin and Fox study involved sex and sadism. The need to dominate and control was a common theme, both in the manner of the murders (such as the choice of vulnerable victims and the use of torture) and in the murderer's life style (such as infatuation with powerful automobiles and aspirations for a career in law enforcement). Although multiple murderers may have a criminal record, they are not typical hardened criminals. Serious psychiatric disorder was rarely present in the Levin and Fox sample, though antisocial personality disorder was common, with the murderers appearing to be "extraordinarily normal" in demeanor.

Levin's and Fox's data indicated a lower rate of serial and mass murder in rural areas and in the South, the latter being a surprise because the general murder rate is very high in the South. (Serial and mass murder seem to be most common in the West, particularly in California.) Like Lunde, Levin and Fox grouped serial and mass murderers together in their study and this reduces the validity of their conclusions.

Federal Bureau of Investigation

The Federal Bureau of Investigation published an analysis of a mixed group of 25 serial and 11 single or double sexual murderers (FBI, 1985; Burgess et al., 1986; Ressler et al., 1988). Their birth dates ranged from 1904 to 1958, though most were born in the 1940s and 1950s. All were male, most were white and the majority were eldest sons (the first- or second-born child). The majority were pleasant in appearance, with few noticeable physical defects and were average or above-average in intelligence. The majority began life in two-parent homes and poverty was not a common factor.

The families from which the murderers came, however, were somewhat dysfunctional. Half of the families had members with criminal histories and over half had members with psychiatric problems. Over two-thirds of the families had at least one member with an alcohol-abuse problem, one-third had a member who abused drugs and half had a member with a sexual problem. Almost half of the murderers had experienced some geographic relocation and 17 percent had moved frequently. Just over half had their biological father leave home before they had reached the age of 12. Nearly half had spent some time away from home in foster care or in institutions before the age of 18. Two-thirds of the murderers themselves had psychiatric problems early in life. The majority had a mother who was the dominant parent during childhood. Half of the murderers reported a cold or uncaring relationship with their mother and two-thirds reported the same with their father. They typically viewed their parents' discipline as unfair, hostile, abusive and inconsistent. Thirteen reported physical abuse, 12 reported sexual abuse and 23 reported psychological abuse.

As they grew up, the role of fantasy—primarily of the violent and sadistic kind—became important to these men and many had shown cruelty to animals and neighborhood children. Twenty of the men had rape fantasies before they reached the age of 18. Despite their intelligence, the men performed poorly in academic, occupational, military and sexual settings. The majority had poor work histories in mainly unskilled positions. Only four of the 14 who served in the military were given honorable discharges. The majority saw themselves as failures and had low self-esteem. They saw themselves as loners and were insensitive to the needs of others. They saw the world as unjust, desired to be strong, powerful and in control and favored autoerotic sexual activities, especially masturbation.

The fantasies of the men in this sample initially focused on the kill itself, but after the first murder, their attention was centered on improving the various phases of the act. Subsequent killings became more organized as the men gained experience.

Leibman

Leibman (1989) studied four serial murderers and concluded that serial murder was an *ego-dystonic* act. Murders can be *ego-syntonic* (or ego-harmonious), in which case the act is acceptable to the murderer on a conscious level. Murders can also be ego-dystonic, in which case the motives and thoughts and actions surrounding the event are unacceptable to the murderer. He may feel intense guilt after the murder or he may feel that he was somehow "driven" to do the act against his will. Alternatively, he may commit the murder in an altered state of consciousness and have no memory of the act. Leibman noted that some serial killers have difficulty believing that they actually committed the murders after they have been captured and confronted with their crimes.

Leibman noted that the majority of serial killers have been white males, 25 to 35 years old, who murdered white women. Leibman noted the following characteristics in the men in her four cases:

1. cruel and extremely violent parenting
2. rejection by the parents in childhood
3. rejection by members of the opposite sex in adulthood
4. prior contact with the criminal justice system as a juvenile and/or adult
5. prior commitment to a mental health facility
6. aberrant sexual behavior
7. being a loner

One case studied by Leibman was Albert DeSalvo, a.k.a. the Boston Strangler. DeSalvo was raised in the slums of Boston, he was one of six children. His father was a violent-tempered alcoholic who would bring prostitutes home and beat his mother in front of them. He was brutal to DeSalvo as well, at one point even selling him to a farmer in Maine for nine dollars. The family lived in extreme poverty and on welfare and the children were often hungry. The father taught Albert to steal when he was five and by age 12, Albert had been arrested twice for burglary and larceny and was sent to a school for delinquents. After his release, he continued to commit crimes, especially burglarizing homes in which women were sleeping.

DeSalvo joined the Army and married a proper German woman who he met overseas. They had two children and an unhappy marriage. Apparently, DeSalvo had insatiable sexual needs. Unfortunately, his wife disliked sex and would often turn him down. She also insulted him in front of their friends and this made DeSalvo feel rejected. He began to rape women in Germany and continued to do so after returning to America. He was eventually arrested and sent to a state mental hospital. After his release in 1961, DeSalvo's wife refused to have sex with him and at that time he began murdering. He sexually assaulted and killed 13 women and attributed his actions to his frigid and rejecting wife.

Holmes and De Burger

In an early paper, Holmes and De Burger (1985) presented a brief description of the characteristics they felt portrayed serial murderers. They maintained that most were white, aged 25 to 34, intelligent and street-smart, charming and charismatic, but also psychopathic. They noted that some are fascinated by police work and associate with off-duty police officers. They noted also that many were born out of wedlock, were physically and sexually abused as children and later became users of drugs and alcohol. These things seemed to exacerbate their sadistic fantasies. They can be intimately involved with women who are unsuspecting of their boyfriend's homicidal activities. They can also have sadistic relationships with their partners.

Holmes and De Burger (1988) later presented another list of common characteristics of serial murders. The typical serial murderer, they say, is a white man, 25 to 35, who typically kills white women. Most serial murders are one-on-one. The victim is typically a stranger to the murderer or at most a slight acquaintance. The primary motive is the kill itself (rather than passion, personal gain or profit) and the victims do not play any role in precipitating their deaths. The motivations are intrinsic—that is, they originate within the murderer himself. Holmes and De Burger argued that a professional hit man operates from an extrinsic motive (namely money) and so should not be considered a true serial murderer. Other researchers prefer to see the professional hit man as simply another type of serial murderer. Serial murders are not usually judged "insane" and are rarely economically deprived.

Holmes and De Burger hypothesized that the most common psychiatric problem among serial murderers is an antisocial personality disorder. This disorder, for which the labels "psychopath" and "sociopath" used to be common, is characterized by having no shame, guilt or remorse for one's antisocial actions. Affected individuals are often quite intelligent and charming and are free from psychosis and neurosis. They are good at manipulating people for their own ends and they prefer to have superficial relationships with others rather than close and intimate friendships. They have almost no capacity to put themselves in the place of their victims and, therefore, have no sympathy for them.

Sears

Sears (1991) reviewed the scholarly literature on serial murderers and noted the following characteristics: (1) they were raised in homes where stability and nurturance were lacking; (2) they often suffered from physical injuries or handicaps; (3) they never developed a sense of self-worth; (4) they turned to day-dreaming and fantasies as a way to break free from their unpleasant environment, fantasies that eventually centered upon sex and violence; (5) they are incapable of forming long-lasting meaningful relationships as adults; (6) they adopt a facade of normalcy; (7) they appear to be free of severe psychiatric disorder; (8) they are quite intelligent and are often perceived as successful in their academic and professional lives despite a mediocre or poor performance record; (9) they are self-centered and have a need for attention from others; (10) they started to commit their crimes in their twenties or early thirties; (11) they are fascinated by (and sometimes obsessed with) police work yet see the police as incompetent bunglers; (12) they are quite energetic and require very little sleep; and (13) they often use alcohol or drugs prior to committing their crimes.

Hazelwood, Dietz and Warren

Hazelwood, Dietz and Warren (1992; see also Dietz et al., 1990) studied 30 male sexually sadistic criminals, 17 of whom were serial killers. Twenty-nine were white and fewer than a half had post-high-school education. About half used drugs or alcohol, one-third had been in the armed forces and 43 percent were married at the time they committed their offenses. Fifty-seven percent had no criminal record.

Forty-three percent of the men had engaged in homosexual activity as adults, 20 percent in cross-dressing, and 20 percent committed other sexual offenses such as voyeurism and exhibition-ism. Seventy-seven percent bound their victims and 60 percent held them captive for more than 24 hours. The most common sexual assault was anal rape, followed in frequency by forced fellatio, vaginal rape and foreign-object penetration. Two-thirds of the men used at least three of these four acts. Sixty percent of the offenders beat their victims. Twenty-two of the men killed a total of 187 victims; 17 killed three or more people apiece.

Twenty-nine of the men preyed only on white victims and 83 percent of the victims were strangers to the offender. The majority chose female victims, but one-quarter chose men exclusively. Sixteen percent attacked only children, while 26 percent attacked both children and adults.

More than half of the men kept records such as calendars and diaries of their offenses, and 43 percent took and kept personal items such as jewelry and photographs from their victims. None of them kept parts of their victims' bodies, though some kept the entire corpse temporarily or permanently.

About half of the men had parents who were divorced or had affairs. Seven of the men had been physically abused in childhood and six had been sexually abused. Nine had had incestuous relations with their children. Four had made suicide attempts and nine were police "buffs."

In only five of the 30 cases was there evidence that the victims resembled someone significant in the murderer's life. For example, one man who had been married to a woman with long black hair murdered women with long black hair and he referred to these murders as practice for what he would do to his ex-wife.

Since anal and oral rape was preferred by the men over vaginal rape, Dietz and co-workers (1990) suggested that this might result from the common history of homosexual involvement (though they did not test this hypothesis on their sample), or perhaps the murderers viewed anal and oral intercourse as a more degrading and humiliating attack on their female victims.

Dietz and his colleagues noted the complete lack of empathy felt by the murderers toward their victims. They suggested that these men might be diagnosed as having narcissistic or psychopathic personality disorder. Many of the men were interpersonally exploitive and grandiose. They responded to criticism with rage and demanded admiration from others. In addition they often viewed themselves as "supercriminals." These traits would suggest a narcissistic or psychopathic personality.

Hickey

Hickey (1991) collected case studies of 34 women and 169 men who were involved in 159 serial murder cases in the United States from 1795 to 1988. Several of the serial murders involved multiple offenders—37 percent had a partner in the crimes. The 203 serial murderers were responsible for killing between 1,483 and 2,161 victims.

The incidence of murder increased over the period studied—from 0.56 cases per year between 1900 and 1924 to 4.21 cases per year between 1975 and 1988. (Data from the earlier years in the period studied are probably less reliable.) However, the number of victims per case appears to have declined—from 13 to 18 per case between 1900 and 1924 to 7 to 10 per case between 1975 and 1988. In recent years, the most dramatic increase has been in the serial killing of strangers; the serial killing of acquaintances and family members shows a much less marked increase. Of the total sample of 203 serial murderers studied, 7 percent murdered only family members. The female killers were more likely to kill family members (26 percent) than were the males (3 percent). In recent years, only 3 percent of the serial killers murdered family members.

The most common victims were, in order of frequency:

1. Family members, children, husbands, wives and in-laws.
2. Acquaintances, friends and neighbors, children, women who were alone (such as waitresses and prostitutes) and adult males.
3. Strangers, young women alone, children, travelers, people at home and hospital patients.

With regard to the age of the victim, 6 percent of the serial murderers killed only children, 2 percent killed only teenagers and 43 percent only adults (12 percent killed only the elderly). The rest killed victims from different age groups. The percentage of serial murderers that targeted the elderly has increased in recent years, up to 21 percent for the period 1975 to 1988.

Thirty-one percent of the serial murderers targeted only women, 21 percent only men and 48 percent both. For the period 1975 to 1988, the percentage of serial murderers who targeted only women was 37 percent. In only 21 percent of the cases the victims were thought to have played a large role in precipitating their own death.

Hickey felt that the more populous and urban states had more serial murderers, but he did not calculate rates for each state, relying solely on the absolute number of serial murderers. California had the most serial murderers for the period 1795 to 1988, followed by Florida, Illinois, New York and Texas. Iowa and Maine had none.

The median length of the period that serial murderers continued to kill was 4.3 years—8.4 years for the female murderers and 4.2 years for the men. Only 10 percent of the murderers were black, though for the period 1975 to 1988 this percentage rose to 21 percent. Twenty-eight percent of the offenders committed the murders in several states, 45 percent in a limited region and 27 percent in a specific location (such as in their home or place of business). In recent years, the percentage of those who kill in a limited region has increased.

Hickey also focused on the murder of children in his sample. Of the 203 serial murderers he looked at, 31 percent had killed at least one child. Of these serial murderers, 73 percent had killed at least one girl and 68 percent at least one boy. Nearly half of these serial murderers were the parent of the child, and female killers predominated in this activity. The most common motive for male serial killers was sexual gratification followed by enjoyment. The most common motive for female killers was monetary gain, closely followed by enjoyment.

Examining the serial murderers by sex, Hickey noted that most female serial murderers acted alone and used less violent methods than men, for example, poisoning. They tended to kill more victims than male killers did and they were slightly older. Their most common occupation was "homemaker." Very few had prior criminal records and all were white. It has become more common for female serial murderers to target strangers in recent years. The media has tended to give them less terrifying names—"Angel of Death" or "Black Widow" rather than those given to male killers such as the "Ripper" or "Strangler." In 12 percent of the cases studied by Hickey, the murderers were never apprehended, 3 percent were killed by police, 12 percent were executed and 67 percent were confined in prisons or mental hospitals.

The male serial killers generally were blue-collar or unskilled workers and were not highly educated. Their acts tended to be brutal—55 percent mutilated their victims. An analysis of a subsample of the men revealed that about 60 percent had a history of criminal behavior: 43 percent had been incarcerated previously in a prison or mental institution; 7 percent had prior histories of murder, 23 percent robbery and 21 percent burglary; and 35 percent had committed sex-related crimes. Sixty percent had felt rejection from their parents, 23 percent had divorced parents, 23 percent lived in poverty, 13 percent were adopted, 10 percent had been sexually abused and 8 percent were born out of wedlock.

The men tended to be treated more harshly by the criminal justice system than the women. Of those apprehended, 20 percent of the men were executed compared to 14 percent of the women; 14 percent of the men were on death row compared to 3 percent of the women; 45 percent of the men were confined in prisons or mental institutions versus 65 percent of the women. Only one of the 157 men had escaped and one other was free.

In recent years, cases involving "team killers" (serial murderers who work as a team) have become increasingly common. Of the 203 killers studied, 77 worked in teams. About a third of the teams involved people who were related, most commonly married couples and fathers and sons, although brothers, mothers and sons and whole families were also found. Two-thirds of the teams involved nonrelatives, most commonly with a male in command. Only eight of the teams (15 percent of the total team offenders) were heterosexual lovers and another eight were homosexual lovers. These teams were responsible for about 20 percent of the victims in Hickey's sample and the teams killed an average of 12 victims compared to 13 for the solo killers.

The male team killers appeared to be a little more likely to come from unstable homes (i.e., temporary family separations, alcoholic parents, prostitute mothers, parents with prison records and psychiatric problems) than the male solo killers, but they less often reported feelings of rejection by their significant others.

Hickey made an effort to construct a list of serial murderers from other nations. He listed 82 people based on records dating from 1400, 76 of them between 1795 and 1988, the period for the 203 American killers he studied. Twenty percent were females. The European nations with the most serial murderers were Great Britain with 26, Germany with 15 and France with nine, but this may reflect the more accurate crime statistics in these nations and the ease of acquiring information.

Jenkins

Jenkins (1989) examined 24 cases of extreme serial murder (10 or more victims) in the United States between 1900 and 1940. He noted that in five of these cases the murderer killed for gain, to claim an inheritance or for insurance money. This type of serial murderer is much less common today. Jenkins suggests that the easy availability of poisons in the first part of the century, combined with the unsophisticated and often careless investigation practices of insurance companies, made this type of serial murder easier to commit.

Rappaport

Rappaport (1988) focused on the sexually sadistic murderer and reported his clinical impressions. Sexual sadists seemed to be motivated by sexual desires, but Rappaport disputed this contention, arguing that neither sexual activity nor murder was the true motive for their behavior. Such murders, he held, are an attempt to cope with an internal conflict, a way to achieve a relief from psychological pain, primarily by demonstrating power and mastery over others.

These killers, Rappaport claimed, are primarily white males in their twenties and thirties; they are intelligent, personable, sociable and seldom have criminal records. They suffer from gender-identity conflicts and a sense of purposelessness. The latter results in frequent changes in jobs, location, roles and goals. Their histories usually include alcohol and drug abuse, physical and sexual abuse and parents who died or divorced. Rappaport suggested a common finding of a borderline personality disorder diagnosis and alcohol intoxication—problems that often lead to further uncontrolled behavior.

James

James (1991) examined the cases of 28 serial murderers and concluded that the majority were white, between the ages of 28 and 38, were average or above-average in intelligence and had criminal records. About half of them were thieves. They typically showed no remorse for their crimes. The majority used a knife to commit murder, though many also carried a gun.

The profile suggested by James was a male, often the oldest boy in the family, whose father left home before he reached puberty. The mother was either weak or emasculating. As a boy, he tortured animals and wet his bed. His performance in school was below his potential and he frequently dropped out before graduating from high school. Additionally, he did not get along well with his peers. If he joined the service, he was typically discharged because of poor adjustment. He did not relate well to women, masturbated excessively and engaged in a great deal of fantasy.

His victims were most often strangers he approached in a car or on a motorcycle that was registered to himself or to a relative. He used a "con game" or ruse to get the victim to go to a place so that he could attack her. He usually stripped the victim of all or part of her clothing and after killing her, he moved the body for disposal and tried to conceal it.

Serial Murderers in England

Jenkins (1988) studied 12 criminals who committed serial murders in England between 1940 and 1985. The majority chose young women, especially those who were prostitutes. Their next victims of choice were children. Most of the serial murderers started their careers at a late age—the median age was 33—and the average age at capture was 36. They murdered an average of four victims a year. Little periodicity was observed and Jenkins concluded that opportunity rather than periodic compulsions accounted for the timing of the murders. The rate of killing did, however, increase over time.

Half were married at the time they committed their first murder, and they usually had stable family relationships and stable living situations. Half had served in the armed forces and a quarter had served in a police constabulary.

Female Serial Murderers

Many writers on the topic of serial murder claim that there have been no female serial murderers. (E.W. Hickey, whose work is reviewed above, is an exception as is Segrave [1992] who listed 84 cases of women who were serial or mass murderers from around the world between 1580 and 1990.)

According to Segrave, the average female multicidal killer commits her first murder at age 31 and continues to kill for five years before being apprehended. The average number of victims is 17. Most murders take place in the home of the killer and often the murderer and victim share a residence. Her most popular murder weapon is arsenic.

The majority of the victims were from the murderer's immediate and extended family, while other victims had close ties to her as employers, friends or suitors. A large percentage of the victims are powerless, such as children or the very elderly and the sick (such as nursing home patients). During the murdering period, there are indications that all is not well with the murderer and neighbors often gossip about the suspect's behavior. After arrest and conviction, the female murderer typically shows little remorse, is usually judged as sane and is sentenced to a long prison term.

Of the 84 female subjects Segrave studied, 35 used poison and 30 used arsenic to kill their victims, and stabbing and cutting were the next most common methods. There were very few mass murderers such as Charles Whitman who killed people at random in the street and few sexually motivated murderers like Ted Bundy. Several of the women murdered travelers and patients in nursing homes for money, or killed for insurance money.

A few of the women murdered family members. Twelve of the women limited their victims to the family, killing 18 husbands and 29 of their own children, four mothers, one father, four cousins, five in-laws, one brother, one sister, one aunt and one uncle.

Twenty-five of the women murdered three or more of their own children in one single bloody day (and so in terms of the timing of their murders, they are not true serial murderers). Eleven of these women were poor and had marital problems. They used painless methods to kill such as asphyxiation. Eight of these 11 women committed suicide after murdering. The other 14 murderers in this group had psychiatric disorders and six of them committed suicide afterwards. This group of women tended to use more brutal methods when they murdered; one of them threw her children off the top of a building and another hanged her children from a beam in a cellar.

The Psychiatric State of Serial Murderers

There are many views about the psychiatric disorders that characterize serial murderers, but there is no solid research that identifies specific psychiatric conditions in a sample of serial murderers. Thus, we are left only with opinions.

Jenkins (1992), for example, saw serial murderers as either paranoid schizophrenics or sexual psychopaths. Liebert (1985) thought that narcissistic personality disorder was common in serial murderers and both Liebert and Rappaport (1988) suggested that borderline personality disorder was a frequent finding.[*] Vetter (1990)

---

[*] Borderline personality disorder is characterized by difficulties in establishing a secure self-identity, distrust, difficulty in controlling anger and other emotions, and impulsive and self-destructive behavior. Narcissistic personality disorder is characterized by a grandiose sense of self-importance combined with occasional feelings of inferiority. Such people are demanding of others, yet give little in return and show little empathy. They are exploitative of others and have long histories of erratic interpersonal relationships.

discussed the importance of feelings of dissociation, in other words, "the lack of integration of thoughts, feelings and experiences into the stream of consciousness." He noted that amnesia was sometimes present in serial murderers, as it was in the case of Kenneth Bianchi, the "Hillside Strangler," who, along with his cousin Angelo Buono, claimed 10 victims in Los Angeles in 1977. Amnesia is also a major characteristic of multiple personality, which is one type of dissociative disorder. Vetter suggested that dissociative disorders in psychopaths would be especially conducive to serial murder. Brown (1991b) suggested that various serial murderers showed evidence of antisocial personality disorder, sadistic sexual disorder, psychosis, obsessive-compulsive disorder, organicity (the presence of brain damage) and multiple personality disorder. However, none of these authors conducted standardized psychiatric interviews on a sample of serial murderers and, therefore, they were unable to compare their diagnoses with a meaningful comparison group such as murderers who had killed only one person.

Lunde (1976) suggested that serial murderers are not usually psychotic, whereas Karpman (1954) felt that individuals who committed lust murders were nearly always psychotic (and sexually impotent). Danto (1982) thought that serial murderers may have obsessive-compulsive disorders.

Stone (1989) suggested that the condition that characterizes many murderers is a combination of antisocial and narcissistic personality disorders. Individuals with an antisocial personality disorder show no shame, guilt or remorse and often have a chronic history of antisocial and criminal behavior. Individuals with a narcissistic personality disorder are pathologically self-centered and egoistical. Stone suggested the term *malignant narcissism* to express the combination of these two disorders. He suggested that murderers might be arranged on a scale from weak to strong malignant narcissism in the following way:

Level 1: Some murderers feel that they are being chronically humiliated, and are in a constant state of feeling like a "nobody." Mark Chapman, who murdered John Lennon, thought he could convert himself from a nobody into a somebody by killing someone famous.

Level 2: Being fired from a job makes some people feel that they are no longer "respectable." In certain cases, such persons will murder their former employer or co-workers. Sometimes, as in the case of James Huberty (who massacred 21 people at a McDonald's in San Ysidro, California), the victims were innocent bystanders.

Level 3: Rejection by someone who once loved him is a severe injury to a narcissist because the possibility of finding a replacement seems nearly impossible. Robert Herrin killed Bonnie Garland for this reason (Gaylin, 1983).

Level 4: In Level 3 murders, at least the murderer loved the woman he killed. Victims, often family members, may be murdered for reasons other than jealousy or rejected love. Jeffrey McDonald killed his pregnant wife and two daughters out of rage and love did not play a role (McGinniss, 1983).

Level 5: Some murderers kill relatives because they are "in the way"—preventing the murderer from obtaining money or blocking certain opportunities. Diane Downs killed her three children because they were hindering her new romance (Rule, 1987). While not yet determined, speculation is that Susan Smith, who in 1994 allegedly drowned her two young sons by strapping them into their car seats while they were still alive and rolling the car into a river, did so because she was afraid that the man she wanted as a lover would not be interested in her if she had children.

Level 6: Mass murderers serve to define Level 6, especially the "loners" such as Richard Speck who killed eight nurses in 1966.

Level 7: Stone placed the typical serial murderer at Level 7—murderers such as Albert DeSalvo, the Boston Strangler and Peter Sutcliffe, the Yorkshire Ripper in England.

Level 8: Some serial killers have modest interpersonal skills and can relate to certain people in a meaningful way. Other serial killers lack even this ability, with no human feeling. Their cruelty is ego-syntonic. They are true "monsters." Stone suggested that Gary Gilmore (Mailer, 1979) was this type of person. Some of these men are psychotic and they may be prone to paranoid delusions.

Level 9: There are murderers for whom torture assumes major importance, such as John Wayne Gacy who first horribly tortured and then murdered several dozen young teenagers and buried them under the house in which he lived (Cahill, 1986).

Level 10: Stone reserved the final level for those who turn their houses into a private Auschwitz, such as Mensa member Gary Heidnick who chained mentally retarded women to the walls in the basement of his Philadelphia house where he tortured them for very long periods of time. He kept his half-tortured, but not yet dead prisoners right next to those he had killed.

Comparison Between Serial Murderers and Other Murderers

The results reported by Hickey, based on his sample of 203 cases of serial murderers, are striking because they are very different from those reported for murder in general (Lester, 1991). The general murder rate is highest for African Americans, both as murderers and as victims. About 25 percent of the victims of murder in 1985 were female and the peak age range for victimization was between 20 and 29. In 1984, 18 percent of murders were of relatives and friends, 38 percent of acquaintances and only 18 percent of strangers (26 percent were undetermined). Estimates of the percentage of victims playing a role in their own murder run about 25 percent. It can be seen that serial killers are more likely to murder women, older people, strangers and those who play little or no role in precipitating their own death.

Langevin and co-workers (1988) compared 13 sexual killers with 13 nonsexual killers, but unfortunately only two of the sexual killers were serial murderers. They found a number of interesting differences between the two groups of killers. For example, the sex killers were more likely to strangle their victims, but not more likely to employ excessive force or mutilation. The sex killers were less likely to murder in the victim's home or to be provoked by the victim and were more likely to show a fusion of the sexual and aggressive drives. The sex killers were angrier in general, but not specifically at women. The sex killers exhibited more sadism, transvestism and other sexual deviations, but were not more likely to abuse alcohol or drugs than the nonsexual killers. They were more often diagnosed as having a personality disorder and less often found to be depressed. Both exhibited hallucinations and dissociative states, epilepsy, or had prior psychiatric histories, but the sex killers were less likely to have delusions. The sex killers had committed more sexual offenses in the past, but not more nonsexual crimes. The two types showed few differences in violent habits or childhood symptoms of disturbance (such as enuresis or conduct disorders), but the sex killers were a little more likely to have had temper tantrums and to have run away from home when they were younger.

There was not difference in whether they were raised by their natural parents, in their physical health or in intelligence. This is the kind of comparison we need for serial versus single-victim murderers and it is unfortunate that Langevin and his colleagues had only two serial killers in their sample.

Hickey (1991) noted that mass murderers are usually either apprehended or killed by the police, or they commit suicide, or turn themselves in, whereas serial murderers try to avoid detection. On the other hand, some serial murders occasionally stop killing and the possibility remains that some of them may commit suicide (or, alternatively, be incarcerated for other offenses, move to new locations, murder using a different modus operandi, or lose interest in murdering altogether).

Hickey noted also that popular perceptions seem to see mass murderers as "crazier," at least temporarily, than serial murderers. More formally put, serial murderers are less likely to be psychotic than mass murderers (Lunde, 1976). Mass murderers do not appear to kill simply for the enjoyment of committing the crime, or as a recreation or hobby. Rarely do mass murderers become serial murderers or commit a second mass murder and few, if any, serial murderers ever commit a mass murder.

Holmes and Holmes (1992) noted that serial murderers differ from mass murderers in other ways as well. Mass murderers often die at the scene of the crime (by committing suicide or when killed by police officers). Unlike serial killers, the mass murderer is typically described as having a serious psychiatric disturbance. The mass murderer usually is described by acquaintances as an angry and hostile person, whereas the serial murder is more likely to be described as a normally adjusted person. The traits of the victims are of less concern to the mass murderer. His victims are in the wrong place at the wrong time (unless he is killing his family members).

The Style of Serial Murder

Norris (1989) focused on the type of serial killer who receives wide media publicity, such as Carlton Gary who murdered seven elderly women in Columbus, Georgia, in 1977 and 1978 and Robert Long who murdered 10 women, mostly prostitutes, in 1984 in the Tampa Bay area of Florida. He described seven phases through which they pass.

1. *The aura phase* refers to the murderer's state of mind as the

urge to murder grows. In this phase he withdraws from everyday reality and begins to fantasize about his intended act. The aura phase can last minutes or months, during which a few serial murderers can verbalize their feelings and are aware that they are losing contact with reality.

2. *The trolling phase* refers to the search for the victim. The murderer may visit preferred locales, identify the preferred type of victim and then select one. He may then stalk the victim for days or weeks until he is familiar with their routine.

3. *The wooing phase* involves getting to know the victim and winning her confidence. The victim may have to be persuaded to accompany the murderer to the predetermined spot where the assault and murder will take place.

4. *The capture* refers to placing the victim in a position from which she cannot escape. For example, the victim may be tied up or hit until unconscious.

5. *The murder* is the moment of emotional high for most serial killers.

6. *The totem phase* is an attempt to prolong the intensity of the murder itself by various means, including dismembering the body, carrying parts of the dead body away or burying them in symbolic places, photographing or videotaping the murder and the scene, or keeping certain possessions of the victim.

7. *The depression phase* ends the sequence for the murderer for now he must go back to the state of psychological pain and torment in which he lives most of the time. He remains unsatisfied, powerless and depressed until the desire to kill begins to grow and overtake him again.

Modus Operandi

A great deal of work is invested in studying the methods of operation employed by criminals, including serial murderers, to determine whether or not a series of crimes could be committed by a single offender. This is far from easy. Douglas and Munn (1992) presented the case of Nathaniel Cody who was convicted in 1989 of the murder of eight victims between 1984 and 1987.

Cody's first murder victim was a 25-year-old black female who he killed in August 1984. He stabbed her nine times in the chest and slashed her throat. In July 1985, he killed a 15-year-old girl, her mother and two of their male friends. He nearly severed the girl's head from her body. He asphyxiated the mother and left her body draped over the side of the bath tub. Both males were shot and one had his throat slit. His last killing spree took place in August 1987, when Cody killed his grandfather and two nephews aged 8 and 12. The grandfather was stabbed five times in the chest and seven times in the back. The two boys were strangled with a ligature.

In this case, the victims differed considerably from one another and the methods for killing varied. What then was the "signature" of the murderer? Douglas and Munn noted the bloodiness of the killings and the overkill, that is, instead of inflicting one or two decisive stab wounds, Cody stabbed some of his victims repeatedly. Douglas and Munn suggested that this excessive stabbing indicated that Cody had a need to dominate, control and manipulate his victims. Each victim was positioned face down and he forced the mother he killed to watch him murder her daughter. However, the "signature" was the ligatures he used on three of the victims. The ligatures involved an unusual configuration and material. In all three cases, Cody used electrical appliance or telephone cords that he found at the scene, in other words, he did not bring the tying materials with him. He used a handcuff-style configuration, looping each cord around the wrists and ankles and connecting them with a lead going through the legs.

Comment

This review of the characteristics of serial murderers has revealed a great deal of agreement between the different writers. However, there are several problems with their conclusions. First, many of the researchers have grouped serial and mass murderers together despite the fact that these two kinds of murderers appear to be quite different. Future research should separate the different types of murderers. Second, few of the studies employed any comparison group. We need to compare serial murderers with single-victim murderers and mass murderers in order to identify the unique characteristics of each group.

Finally, most researchers have limited themselves to studying sexually motivated serial killers, thereby omitting many other murderers whose killings meet the criteria for serial murder. We need to include *all* serial murderers in any kind of effective research and to identify the characteristics of each type of serial murderer. It is this problem that we deal with in the next chapter.

References

Brown, J.S. The historical similarity of 20th century serial sexual homicide to pre-20th century occurrences of vampirism. *American Journal of Forensic Psychiatry* 12(2):11-24, 1991a.

Brown, J.S. The psychopathology of serial sexual homicide. *American Journal of Forensic Psychiatry* 12(1):13-21, 1991b.

Burgess, A.W., C.R. Hartman, R.K. Ressler, J.E. Douglas and A. McCormack. Sexual homicide. *Journal of Interpersonal Violence* 1:251-272, 1986.

Cahill, T. *Buried Dreams.* New York: Bantam, 1986.

Danto, B.L. A psychiatric view of those who kill. In B.L. Danto, J. Bruhns and H.A. Kutscher (eds.), *The Human Side of Homicide.* New York: Columbia University Press, 1982.

Dickson, G. *Murder by Numbers.* London: Robert Hale, 1958.

Dietz, P.E., R.R. Hazelwood and J. Warren. The sexually sadistic criminal and his offenses. *Bulletin of the American Academy of Psychiatry and the Law* 18:163-178, 1990.

Douglas, J.E. and C. Munn. Violent crime scene analysis. *FBI Law Enforcement Bulletin* 61(2):1-10, 1992.

Federal Bureau of Investigation. The men who murdered. *FBI Law Enforcement Bulletin* 54(8):2-6, 1985.

Gaylin, W. *The Killing of Bonnie Garland.* New York: Penguin, 1983.

Hazelwood, R.R., P.E. Dietz and J. Warren. The criminal sexual sadist. *FBI Law Enforcement Bulletin* 61(2):12-20, 1992.

Hickey, E.W. *Serial Murderers and Their Victims.* Pacific Grove, CA: Brooks/Cole, 1991.

Holmes, R.M. and J.E. De Burger. Profiles in terror. *Federal Probation* 49(3):29-34, 1985.

Holmes, R.M. and S.T. Holmes. Understanding mass murder. *Federal Probation* 56(1):53-61, 1992.

James, E. *Catching Serial Killers.* Lansing, MI: International Forensic Services, 1991.

Jenkins, P. Serial murder in England, 1940-1985. *Journal of Criminal Justice* 16:1-15, 1988.

Jenkins, P. Serial murder in the United States, 1900-1940. *Journal of Criminal Justice* 17:377-397, 1989.

Jenkins, P. A murder "wave"? *Criminal Justice Review* 17(1):1-19, 1992.

Karpman, B. *The Sexual Offender and His Offenses.* New York: The Julian Press, 1954.

Langevin, R., M.H. Ben-Aron, P. Wright, V. Marchese and L. Handy. The sex killer. *Annals of Sex Research* 1:263-301, 1988.

Leibman, F.H. Serial murderers. *Federal Probation* 53(4):41-45, 1989.

Lester, D. *Questions and Answers About Murder.* Philadelphia: The Charles Press, 1991.

Levin, J. and J.A. Fox. *Mass Murder.* New York: Plenum, 1985.

Liebert, J.A. Contributions of psychiatric consultation in the investigation of serial murder. *International Journal of Offender Therapy and Comparative Criminology* 29:187-200, 1985.

Lunde, D.T. *Murder and Madness.* New York: Norton, 1979.

Mailer, N. *The Executioner's Song.* Boston: Little, Brown, 1979.

McGinniss, J. *Fatal Vision.* New York: Putnam, 1983.

Norris, J. *Serial Killers.* New York: Anchor, 1989.

Rappaport, R.G. The serial and mass murderer. *American Journal of Forensic Psychiatry* 9(1):39-48, 1988.

Ressler, R., A.W. Burgess and J.E. Douglas. *Sexual Homicide.* Lexington, MA: D.C. Heath, 1988.

Rule, A. *Small Sacrifices.* New York: New American Library, 1987.

Sears, D. *To Kill Again.* Wilmington, DE: Scholarly Resources, 1991.

Segrave, K. *Women Serial and Mass Murderers.* Jefferson, NC: McFarland, 1992.

Stone, M.H. Murder. *Psychiatric Clinics of North America* 12(3):643-651, 1989.

Vetter, H. Dissociation, psychopathy and the serial murderer. In S.A. Egger (ed.), *Serial Murder.* New York: Praeger, 1990.

Chapter 7

Types of Serial Murderers

To understand the phenomenon of serial murder it is useful to first identify the different types of murderers that exist. One common way of looking at serial murderers is to classify them into categories: crime spree killers, hit men, poisoners, psychotics and sexual sadists (Brown, 1991). However, for categories to be useful as a classificatory scheme, they need to be detailed. For example, it is necessary to know the characteristics of the murderers that fall into each category and the proportions of serial murderers in those categories. Ultimately, what needs to be determined is whether serial murderers can be reliably labeled using these categories. Let us look at several of the more detailed classificatory schemes that have been proposed by researchers.

Rappaport

Rappaport (1988) defined four categories of people who commit multicide: pseudocommandos, family annihilators, set-and-run killers and serial murderers. The first three types will be discussed below in the section on mass murderers. Rappaport described serial murderers as: (1) the crime spree killers who commit a series of murders in one continuous period of criminal behavior; (2) functionaries of organized criminal operations, such as Mafia hit men, terrorists, mercenaries and gang members who are motivated by a cause or by money; (3) custodial poisoners or asphyxiators who are mainly physicians or nurses but also including babysitters and foster parents who kill patients or clients for financial, vengeful or supposedly altruistic reasons; (4) psychotic killers who are responding to hallucinations and delusions when they commit their murderous acts; and (5) sexually sadistic killers.

Dietz

Dietz (1986) suggested the following typology for serial murderers:

1. The psychopathic sexual sadists. Typically, according to Dietz, all of the known serial killers with 10 or more victims have been males who have been diagnosed with an antisocial personality disorder (the modern term for psychopath) and with sexually sadistic tendencies. Examples of this type of killer include Ted Bundy, Dean Corll and John Wayne Gacy.
2. Crime spree killers. These murderers are motivated by the search for excitement, money and valuables. Bonnie Parker and Clyde Barrow ("Bonnie and Clyde") and Charles Stark-weather may be considered crime spree killers.
3. Functionaries of organized criminal operations. This category includes ethnic gangs, prison gangs, street gangs, members of organized crime (the Mafia or La Cosa Nostra), contract killers, illegal mercenaries and terrorists.
4. Custodial poisoners and asphyxiators. These are typically caretakers of the ill or of children and cases involving physicians and nurses have been reported in which medications, such as digitalis, have been administered to a series of patients.
5. Supposed psychotics. These murderers claim to be acting under the influence of hallucinatory voices or delusions. Dietz included the qualifier "supposed" because he was far from sure that a valid case had been described. For example, although David Berkowitz (the "Son of Sam" killer) is typically thought to illustrate this type of serial murderer, some of the details of the case have been contested.

Gee

Gee (1988), a pathologist, was interested in the circumstances of serial murder and he focused particularly on the disposal of the bodies. The first type of serial murderer secretly hides the bodies of victims and tries to conceal the crimes. The absence of the victims from the community is not noticed and their bodies are discovered by chance. A case of this type was Dean Corll who murdered in

Houston in the 1970s. Corll wrapped the bodies of the boys he killed in plastic and buried them under the floor of his candy factory and in the nearby countryside grounds. When these victims are found, it is often hard for pathologists to determine their identity because their remains have decomposed.

The second type of serial murderer kills several people in succession, but the homicidal nature of the deaths is not initially realized by investigators. Gee reported a case of a mentally retarded youth who set fires that killed 26 people over a period of 10 years before the police even suspected arson. The problem for the pathologist in these cases is to identify the deaths as homicide.

The third type of serial murderer makes no attempt to conceal the victims or the fact that these people have been murdered; in fact, very apparent injuries are left that point directly to murder. The most famous case of this type, of course, is Jack the Ripper who killed prostitutes in late-nineteenth-century England. The killer usually slashed his victim's faces and throats and disemboweled them. Sometimes he took parts of their bodies with him and sometimes he left slabs of flesh near the dead body. The police tried everything they could to establish a link between the different murders, but were never able to solve this most notorious serial murder case. In fact, new theories about who Jack the Ripper was have surfaced within the last few years.

Holmes and De Burger

Holmes and De Burger (1988) believe that the factors that cause a person to become a serial murderer are rarely *biogenic* (that is, the result of a brain disorder, biochemical and physiological abnormalities or mental deficiency) or *sociogenic* (the result of growing up in a bad neighborhood, amid economic hardship, in an unstable family and a violent subculture). They believe that the reasons are *psychogenic*, in other words, rooted in the individual minds of the murderers. The classification they propose, therefore, is psychological in nature, based on the behavioral background of the murderer, the methods he uses, the location he chooses and the victims he kills.

Victims may be chosen systematically or at random. For example, a serial murderer may kill any woman who hitches a ride with him or he may only choose victims who have particular traits. For example, most of Ted Bundy's victims were young women with long dark hair that was parted in the middle. Some serial murders are carefully planned, while others are more spontaneous. Some serial murderers pick their victims carefully, identifying and stalking them for hours, days or longer. Related to this is the degree of organization involved. A serial murderer who takes weapons and other implements to the crime scene, plans the murder carefully and takes care to have control over the victim is committing an organized murder. Most victims of serial murderers are strangers, but occasionally relatives may be victims. Nannie Doss, for example, poisoned four of her husbands and seven other family members.

Some serial murderers are act-focused, meaning that their goal is to kill and to get it over with swiftly. Other serial murderers are process-focused; typically, their murders are brutal and sadistic, often involving torture and sexual assault. Process-focused murderers often engage in a great deal of fantasizing before they murder and use excessive violence—they "overkill" when they murder.

Some serial murderers focus on victims from one city or region or they may travel widely. For example, Albert DeSalvo (who many believe was the Boston Strangler) murdered 13 women from the Boston area. Earl Nelson, on the other hand, murdered 20 women in six states, ranging from New York to California. The geographically confined murderer is typically employed in the community and may be well-known and respected (Ted Bundy, for example). Also, the murderer may not display any overt signs of violent tendencies.

Holmes and De Burger proposed four types of serial murderers: visionary, mission-oriented, hedonistic and control-oriented. These are described below:

Visionary Type

The least common type of serial murderer is made up of those who respond to the command to kill by voices or who see visions that demand that they kill certain people or types of people. They may attribute the voices to the Devil or to God. As one might expect, these murderers are often judged to be psychotic. Because these murderers are psychiatrically disturbed, there may be biogenic factors involved.

Holmes and De Burger described Cleo Green as a typical visionary type of serial murderer. In St. Louis, in the summer of 1984, he brutally assaulted four elderly women in their apartments. His first victim was Ida Mae York who he stabbed over 200 times and then decapitated. The other victims were murdered in a similar fashion.

Green was a 26-year-old black male who was unemployed and lived with his mother. He believed that he was possessed by a "red demon" and that the only way he could escape this demon—even if only temporarily—was to murder an elderly woman. This, he believed, would cause the demon to leave him and enter her body. Green was judged incompetent to stand trial and was placed in an institution for the criminally insane.

Mission-Oriented Type

The mission-oriented serial murderer consciously chooses to eliminate a particular group or category of persons who he feels are undesirable or unworthy of living.

Beoria Simmons, a 29-year-old social worker who lived in Louisville, Kentucky, was convinced that prostitutes where sinful and immoral and that it was his mission to cleanse the city of such women. In 1984, he killed a teenager who he assumed was a prostitute. Later, Simmons killed two other women, aged 29 and 39, before he was arrested. He was tried and sentenced to death.

Hedonistic Type

The hedonistic murderer seeks pleasure or thrills when he kills. He may derive pleasure from the kill itself, from the sexual arousal and gratification associated with the event (lust murder), or from the consequences of the murder, such as being free to remarry. There are three subtypes of hedonistic killers: lust-oriented, thrill-oriented and comfort-oriented.

As an example of the lust-oriented killer, Holmes and De Burger presented the case of Gerald Thompson, a factory worker in Peoria, Illinois, who in 1933 abducted and killed 16 women. He kidnapped each woman in the evening, drove them to a deserted area in a car that he had outfitted with locks and chains for transporting his victims, stripped them and tied them to a frame in front of the headlights of his car. He then raped and killed each woman. He was captured in June 1935, found guilty and executed later that year.

To illustrate the thrill-oriented type, Holmes and De Burger presented the case of Christopher Wilder, a rich, handsome, charming and intelligent man. In 1984, he tortured and killed women aged 17 to 24 in several states. The victims were sadistically assaulted, raped, bound and killed by stabbing or strangulation. One victim escaped and reported being beaten, bound, raped, tortured with electrical shocks and having glue poured into her eyes. Wilder, who had prior arrests for sexual assault in the U.S. and Australia, was killed while attempting to escape from the police.

James Watson is an example of the comfort-oriented type of serial murderer. In 1910 in El Centro, California, Watson's wife became convinced that her husband was planning to kill her. She went to the police who brought Watson in for questioning. The police suspected he might already have killed people and let him try to plea bargain by revealing where he had buried his alleged victims. It turned out that Watson had married and then killed 15 women in the prior 10 years, mostly lonely widows with no close relatives and few friends. When asked why he had done this, he said that he married and murdered them for their money.

Holmes and De Burger gave a more detailed analysis of the lust murderer. They distinguished two types: the disorganized asocial type and the organized nonsocial type. The profile of the disorganized asocial type includes the following traits:

below-average intelligence
socially inadequate
does unskilled work
sexually incompetent
low birth-order status
father's work unstable
harsh discipline as a child
anxious mood during crime
minimal use of alcohol
minimal precipitating situational stress
lives alone
lives or works near crime scene
minimal interest in the news coverage of his crime
significant behavior change (drugs, alcohol or religion)

In contrast, the organized nonsocial type has the following traits:

average to above-average intelligence
socially competent
does skilled work
sexually competent
high birth-order status
father's work stable
inconsistent childhood discipline
controlled mood during crime

uses alcohol with the crime
precipitating situational stress
lives with partner
mobile, with a car
follows own crimes in the news
may change jobs or leave town

The crime scenes of these two types differ considerably as the lists below show:

Organized	*Disorganized*
offense planned	spontaneous offense
victim a targeted stranger	victim a random stranger
controlled conversation	minimal conversation
scene reflects control	scene random and sloppy
demands victim be submissive	suddenly violent to victim
restraints used	minimal use of restraints
aggressive prior to death	sex after death
body hidden	body left in view
weapon/evidence absent	weapon/evidence present
transports body	body left at scene

Hazelwood and Douglas (1980) have also discussed the differences between the organized nonsocial type and the disorganized asocial type of sexually motivated murderer in cases where there is sadistic mutilation of the body. The *organized nonsocial type* is indifferent to the interests and welfare of others, but he can appear charming and amiable in order to manipulate others. He is irresponsible and self-centered but he is fully aware of the criminal nature of his actions. He commits the attack in a secluded place and then moves the body to a location where it can be found. He is excited by the publicity surrounding the discovery of the body. He takes his weapons to the scene of the crime, removes them afterwards and often mutilates and tortures the victim prior to death. He may have intercourse with the victim both prior to and after the murder. This type of murderer may dissect the body in order to hinder the identification of the victim. He may return to the scene of the crime to see if the body has been discovered and to check on the progress of the investigation. He may even hang out with the police in order to be informed about the investigation.

The *disorganized asocial type* is a loner and has difficulty with interpersonal relationships. He often feels lonely and rejected by others. His criminal actions are more frenzied and less methodical than those committed by the organized nonsocial type (the victim's blood is often found on the murderer's clothes) and he murders close to his place of residence or work. He leaves the body at the scene of the crime and makes no attempt to conceal it. He uses a weapon of opportunity and may leave it at the scene of the crime. He may dissect the body out of curiosity. Rather than having intercourse with the victim, he may insert objects into the body orifices, sometimes brutally. Eating parts of the victim is more characteristic of this type of murderer. He may return to the scene of the crime to mutilate the victim further or simply to relive the experience.

Both these types of murderer were probably abused and neglected as children. The disorganized asocial type develops a poor self-image, rejects the society that he feels has rejected him and he may be suicidal. Family and friends will describe him as a quiet person who keeps to himself. During adolescence he may have shown deviant sexual behavior such as spying on women (voyeurism) and stealing women's clothes (fetishism) because he lacks the self-confidence to approach women in a normal fashion. In contrast, the organized nonsocial type externalizes his aggression rather than internalizing it and usually was a troublemaker during adolescence, frequently having problems with family, friends and authority figures.

Control-Oriented Type

The gratification for the control-oriented murderer comes from having power over the victims, especially the "thrill" of deciding whether a person will live or die, and how and when. If a sexual assault occurs, the primary motive is achieving complete control, whereas with the hedonistic type, sexual pleasure is more important.

Randall Woodfield, "The I-5 Killer" who operated in Oregon and Washington in early 1980s, had been an outstanding football player at college, but he failed to make it in professional football. He dealt with his loss of hero status by assaulting and murdering women, committing some 60 rapes and killing 12 to 18 young women along Interstate 5 before being captured.

Predatory Type

Holmes (1990) described a fifth type of serial murderer whom he called the *predator*. This person hunts humans in order to kill them as a form of recreation, rather than for achieving tranquility or omnipotence.

Holmes and De Burger (1988) summarized the differences between these four types in a simple table (see Table 1) and Holmes (1989) suggested further differences, shown in Table 2.

Typologies for Women

Holmes and Holmes (1994) adapted their typology for female serial murderers, listing five types: visionary, comfort-oriented, hedonistic, power-seeking and disciple. Female *visionary types* are the same as that described in connection with male serial murderers. Whereas in his earlier typology Holmes listed the *comfort-oriented type* as one kind of hedonistic murderer, in his later typology for women he separates them: the female comfort type denotes murderers who kill for material gain, such as insurance money, and the *hedonistic type* denotes those whose sexual gratification comes from violence. The female *power-seeking type* resembles the control-oriented type found in the male serial murderers. An additional type assigned to women is the *disciple*, which describes persons who have fallen under the spell of a charismatic leader and kill on command. The pay-off for this type of murderer is pleasing the leader. The characteristic features of the crimes of female murderers are shown in Table 3

Mass Murderers

Holmes and Holmes (1992) proposed a typology of the mass murderer and it is interesting to note that the typology differs significantly from that proposed for the serial murderer. The *disciple* kills because ordered to do so by a charismatic leader such as Charles Manson. The *family annihilator* murders his entire family at one time and is typically the senior male in the family who has a history of depression and alcohol abuse. The *pseudocommando* stockpiles weapons and then plans a one-man raid on a specific place, such as James Huberty's shooting of 21 people at the McDonald's restaurant in San Ysidro, California in 1984. The *disgruntled employee* goes to his former workplace and kills supervisors and co-workers at random. In 1986, Patrick Sherrill returned to the Oklahoma post office where he had worked, looking for his supervisors but shooting anyone he came across in the process. He shot 14 co-workers. Finally, Holmes and Holmes described the *set-and-run* mass murderer who may plant

Table 1
A Typology of Male Serial Killers

	visionary	mission-oriented	hedonistic			control-oriented
			lust	thrill	comfort	
Victims						
specific	no	yes	yes	no	no	yes
nonspecific	yes	no	no	yes	yes	no
random	yes	no	yes	yes	no	no
nonrandom	no	yes	no	yes	yes	yes
known	no	no	no	no	yes	no
stranger	yes	yes	yes	yes	no	yes
Methods						
act-focused	yes	yes	no	no	yes	no
process-focused	no	no	yes	yes	no	yes
planned*	no	yes	yes	no	yes	yes
spontaneous	yes	no	no	yes	no	no
organized*	no	yes	yes	no	yes	yes
disorganized	yes	no	no	yes	no	no
Location						
concentrated	yes	yes	yes	no	yes	no
dispersed	no	no	no	yes	no	yes

* Note that the classifications for planned/spontaneous and organized/disorganized methods are identical. Adapted from R.M. Holmes and J. De Burger, *Serial Murder* (Beverly Hills, CA: Sage), 1988. Note that the traits listed for each type are different in Holmes' 1994 study, *Murder in America.*

a bomb in a building or put poisoned bottles of aspirin or soft drinks in a supermarket and then await the deaths from a distance.

Jenkins

Jenkins (1988) studied 12 English serial murderers over the period 1940 to 1985 and noted two types. The *predictable type* (represented by four men) had a significant record of juvenile crime, including cruel and violent behavior. All had violent fantasies and were attracted to marital arts and the German Nazis. Most began to murder at an early age and fit the label of "born to kill."

The *respectable type* (represented by eight men) had a few prior

Table 2

A Typology of Male Serial Killers

	visionary	mission-oriented	hedonistic			control-oriented
			lust	thrill	comfort	
controlled crime scene	no	yes	yes	yes	yes	yes
overkill	yes	no	yes	no	no	no
chaotic crime scene	yes	no	no	no	no	no
evidence of torture	no	no	yes	yes	no	yes
body moved	no	no	yes	yes	no	yes
specific victim	no	yes	yes	yes	yes	yes
weapon at scene	yes	no	no	no	yes	no
relational victim	no	no	no	no	yes	no
victim known	yes	no	no	no	yes	no
violent weapon	yes	yes	yes	yes	no	yes
aberrant sex	no	no	yes	yes	no	yes
necrophilia	yes	no	yes	no	no	yes
weapon of torture	no	no	yes	yes	no	no
strangulation	no	no	yes	yes	no	yes
penile penetration	?	yes	yes	yes	yes	yes
object penetration	yes	no	yes	yes	yes	no

Adapted from R.M. Holmes. *Profiling Violent Crimes* (Newbury Park, CA: Sage), 1989.

Table 3
A Typology of Female Serial Killers

	visionary	*comfort*	*hedonistic*	*disciple*	*power*
Victims					
specific	no	yes	yes	no	yes
nonspecific	yes	no	no	yes	no
random	yes	no	yes	no	no
nonrandom	no	yes	no	yes	yes
affiliative	no	yes	no	no	no
stranger	yes	no	yes	yes	yes
Methods					
act-focused	yes	no	no	yes	yes
process-focused	no	yes	yes	no	no
planned*	no	yes	yes	yes	yes
spontaneous	yes	no	no	no	no
organized*	no	yes	yes	yes	yes
disorganized	yes	no	no	no	no
Location					
concentrated	yes	yes	no	no	no
dispersed	no	no	yes	yes	yes

* Note that the classifications for planned/spontaneous and organized/disorganized methods are identical. Adapted from R.M. Holmes and S.T. Holmes, *Murder in America* (Thousand Oaks, CA: Sage), 1994.

arrests for petty theft, embezzlement or forgery, but no violent crime before their twenties. Their minor psychopathological tendencies seemed to be under control until the onset of a major mid-life crisis in which alcohol abuse played a role, and then the murders began.

The Federal Bureau of Investigation

The FBI has also been interested in the distinction between organized and disorganized serial murderers (FBI, 1985b; Ressler et al., 1986). In a sample of 36 sexually motivated murderers, many of whom were serial murderers, they classified 24 as organized (with 97 victims) and 12 as disorganized (with 21 victims). Holmes and De Burger (1988) and the FBI agree completely with each other regarding asocial and nonsocial, organized and disorganized sexual murderers and the difference between their crime scenes.

Sharing Serial Murder

Jenkins (1990) noted that some serial murderers kill in pairs (and some in larger groups). He studied whether the accomplices of serial murderers tend to have a distinct personality and how murderers draw the accomplice under their influence. In the United States between 1971 and 1990, Jenkins identified 58 cases of serial murder in which 10 or more victims were killed, of which 12 appeared to have involved multiple offenders.

Jenkins suggested a typology of these group serial murderers: (1) one dominant and one submissive partner (though Jenkins subdivided this type taking into account the gender of the partners); (2) equally dominant partners; (3) extended family or associational groups; and (4) formalized or ritualized clans or societies.

Some cases seem to involve one person beginning a murder career and later initiating a partner into murder. Other cases involve a joint decision to begin killing. Jenkins felt that group serial murderers are overwhelmingly hedonists, to use the typology developed by Holmes, especially the lust-murderers.

Jenkins also noted that several aspects of contemporary society might have encouraged the appearance of group serial killers; for example, the taste for multiple-partner sex, as evidenced by mate-swapping and by the sharing of partners portrayed in pornographic books and videos. Dominance and submission also figure prominently in modern pornography. In some cases, group serial murder developed as an extension of deviant sexual acts. In California in 1980, Douglas Clark (the Sunset Strip Killer) and Carol Bundy engaged in increasingly deviant sexual behavior with prostitutes which did not violate the taboos against violence and murder. Gradually, however, the sexual mistreatment of the prostitutes evolved into murder. Kenneth Bianchi, the "Hillside Strangler" of California during the late 1970s, also gradually moved from dominating prostitutes to murdering them.

Jenkins noted that other group serial killers, such as John Lesko and Michael Travaglia, active in Pennsylvania in 1979 and 1980, started by beating and robbing homosexuals, perhaps as a way of expressing their masculine prowess. After one excessively violent incident led to murder, they went on a killing spree.

Jenkins suggested that the phenomenon of group serial murder requires sociological explanations in addition to the psychological and psychiatric theories normally applied to serial killers. Jenkins thought that the notion of a subculture of recreational homicide was a useful concept. He modelled his idea on the "subculture of violence" proposed by Wolfgang and Ferracuti (1969) as an explanation for the high incidence of violence, including murder, found in some regions of the world and some subgroups of society and the delinquent subcultures described by Cohen (1955).

Henry Lee Lucas claimed to have killed several hundred people between 1976 and 1982, but the actual figure is probably closer to 10. At first, he traveled and murdered with Ottis Toole, who was Lucas' homosexual lover. He also traveled with Toole's niece, 13-year-old Becky Lorraine Powell, another of Lucas' lovers, whom he eventually murdered. Jenkins considers how this group might have developed and shared common values and beliefs which justified their actions. Perhaps these values are explicit inversions of the normal world which the murderers had come to resent and even hate. Or perhaps each member of the group has normal values but believes that he is deviant from the rest of the group and, therefore, overacts in the deviant role in order to prove himself to the others.

An Attempt at Assessing Reliability

The FBI (1985a) presented crime scenarios for 64 actual murders to six judges in their Behavioral Science Unit. The judges were asked to determine the classification of each scene as either a sexual homicide, a nonsexual homicide, or as unknown. They agreed with the officer who presented the case in 81 percent of the cases. They were then asked to classify each scene as organized, disorganized, mixed or unknown. They agreed with the presenting officers in 74 percent of the cases. Although the classifications examined in this study were simple, the study is the first and only test of the reliability of some elements of a typology.

Comment

Though provocative, the typology proposed by Holmes and De Burger has not been tested. To test a typology, three tasks must be undertaken. First, a set of case studies must be prepared and presented to at least two judges who then classify each case. Once this has been done, the researcher can then calculate the degree of agreement and disagreement in their classifications. Second, there will always be cases that cannot be classified into any of the categories that have been proposed. The percentage of unclassifiable cases must be calculated. Third, some cases are inevitably "mixed" types, that is, they may fit into two or more of the categories. Again, the percentage of mixed types must be calculated.

Although Holmes and De Burger say that they based their typology on 110 serial murderers, they provide none of the required statistics and calculations. Thus, their typology and those of others, must be considered as speculative at the present time.

References

Brown, J.S. The historical similarity of 20th century serial sexual homicide to pre-20th century occurrences of vampirism. *American Journal of Forensic Psychiatry* 12(2):11-24, 1991.

Cohen, A. *Delinquent Boys*. Glencoe, IL: Free Press, 1955.

Dietz, P.E. Mass, serial and sensational homicides. *Bulletin of the New York Academy of Medicine* 62:477-491, 1986.

Federal Bureau of Investigation. Classifying sexual homicide crime scenes. *FBI Law Enforcement Bureau* 54(8):13-17, 1985a.

Federal Bureau of Investigation. Crime scene and profile characteristics of organized and disorganized murderers. *FBI Law Enforcement Bulletin* 54(8):25, 1985b.

Gee, D.J. A pathologist's view of multiple murder. *Forensic Science International* 38:53-65, 1988.

Hazelwood, R.R. and J.E. Douglas. The lust murderer. *FBI Law Enforcement Bulletin* 49(4):18-22, 1980.

Holmes, R.M. *Profiling Violent Crimes*. Newbury Park, CA: Sage, 1989.

Holmes, R.M. Human hunters. *Knightbeat* 9(1):43-47, 1990.

Holmes, R.M. and J. De Burger. *Serial Murder*. Beverly Hills, CA: Sage, 1988.

Holmes, R.M. and S.T. Holmes. Understanding mass murder. *Federal Probation* 56(1):53-61, 1992.

Holmes, R.M. and S.T. Holmes. *Murder in America*. Thousand Oaks, CA: Sage, 1994.

Jenkins, P. Serial murder in England, 1940-1985. *Journal of Criminal Justice* 16:1-15, 1988.

Jenkins, P. Sharing murder. *Journal of Crime and Justice* 12:125-148, 1990.

Rappaport, R.G. The serial and mass murderer. *American Journal of Forensic Psychiatry* 9(1):39-48, 1988.

Ressler, R.K., A.W. Burgess, J.E. Douglas, C.R. Hartman and R.B. D'Agostino. Sexual killers and their victims. *Journal of Interpersonal Violence* 1:288-308, 1986.

Wolfgang, M. and F. Ferracuti. *The Subculture of Violence*. New York: Tavistock, 1969.

Chapter 8

Theories of Serial Murder

The issues raised by the serial murderer are not new to criminological theory. Scholars have long studied sadistic and sexually motivated murderers (for example, Krafft-Ebing, 1892) and modern analyses of these murderers are common (for example, Brittain, 1970; Schlesinger and Revitch, 1983). However, until recent times scholars have not focused on the serial nature of many criminal acts.

Caputi (1987) sees the serial killer as merely an extreme in the latest expression of male supremacy which has always involved the raping and killing of women. One of the clearest examples of this was the case of Marc Lépine who, on December 6, 1989, entered the School of Engineering building at the University of Montréal with a semi-automatic rifle and murdered 14 women and injured 13 others. He walked into a classroom and ordered the men out of the room, lined the women against a wall and began shooting to kill, yelling, "You are all feminists!" Brickman (1992) suggested that Lépine's social statement seemed to be that women are responsible for the failures of men, that women who stand in the way of men's success deserve to be punished and that successful women have abdicated their right to protection. She saw Lépine's act as part of the prevailing tendency of misogynist men to frighten, harm, marginalize and control women as a short-cut to self-advancement. It can be generally stated that men who harm women, whether by physical abuse or by serial murder, gain sexual pleasure, reduction of tension and anger and interpersonal control. They also gain notoriety. In Canada, Marc Lépine's name will be remembered. The 14 women he killed remain anonymous.

Leyton (1986, 1989) saw serial murders as a personalized form of social protest in which killings are an act of revenge by the killer for what he perceives as his social exclusion from society. Serial and mass murderers, according to Leyton, are alienated men who feel trapped in and tired of living dull lives. They also feel as though they live in a culture that, through the mass media, legitimizes violence as a response to frustration. If they no longer wish to live, they stage a mass killing that culminates in their own death; if they wish to live and achieve notoriety, they carry out a series of murders with which they can also settle old scores in a manner that yields sexual pleasure and defies the law and society.

There are, of course, many possible theories of murder that may be applicable to serial murderers. One problem with testing such theories is that often the writers of case studies of serial murderers have little knowledge of the theories and are, therefore, ignorant about which characteristics to look for before writing up the case. However, several writers have presented cases that illustrate a theory of serial murder or offered their opinions on the causes of serial murder based on their clinical experience. Let us examine some of these ideas.

Sears

Sears (1991) reviewed theories of violence to determine whether they provided appropriate explanations for serial murder. He noted that serial killers are commonly diagnosed as psychopaths. One characteristic of the *primary psychopath* is that he is does not experience fear, anxiety or guilt. In contrast, serial killers often experience mounting tension and anxiety before murdering. Primary psychopaths are often impulsive and incapable of planning criminal activity successfully; they cannot tolerate routine and they tend to engage in hastily planned actions that provide immediate gratification. None of these characteristics are found in the majority of serial killers.

The *secondary psychopath* commits antisocial acts because of emotional conflicts or inner distress and he often appears to experience fear and anxiety. Such people are often labeled as acting-out neurotics or neurotic delinquents. This diagnosis appears to fit serial killers better, but whereas secondary psychopaths may feel guilt and remorse after their criminal acts, most serial killers do not. Serial killers appear, therefore, to be a hybrid mix of primary and secondary psychopathic behavior.

Sears noted that psychopaths need thrills and excitement and perhaps this makes it more likely that they will turn to criminal acts in order to obtain this gratification. Sears hypothesizes that because serial killers have this need for excitement, they cannot be satisfied with minor crimes and therefore they resort to more and more brutal acts to satisfy their needs.

Lunde (1979) described two types of multiple murderers—paranoid schizophrenics and sexual sadists. Sears felt that serial killers are more likely to be sexual sadists. In many of these individuals, at some point in their childhood, sexual and aggressive desires seem to have merged, but Sears noted that we lack an understanding of why this happens, especially because some individuals develop sadistic behavior and never feel the need to kill. Possibly, serial killers have not achieved emotional maturity, and therefore have difficulty dealing with their violent and sadistic fantasies in appropriate ways. However, this again leaves us with the problem of trying to understand why these murderers developed in this way. What were the factors that impeded their maturation? Unfortunately, the statistical rarity of serial murder, even among murderers and certainly among the general population, makes it difficult to isolate the particular childhood experiences that could lead to the development of such a rare behavior.

Experience of a brutal and abusive childhood increases the risk of violence in the adult, perhaps by imitation and modeling and perhaps because of the enormous amount of frustration and anger that builds up in abused children. As adults, abused children typically have problems relating intimately to others and they are prone to violent outbursts. They have low self-esteem and lack basic social skills. Toch (1969) noted that people who were abused as children tend to manipulate others through violence in order to satisfy personal needs and tend to be violent whenever they feel threatened. Sears pointed out that both of these behaviors can be found in serial killers. But what links violence to sexual behavior?

Some serial killers have necrophiliac tendencies (that is, sexual attraction to corpses), but necrophilia is quite uncommon and we have little idea as to how such desires develop. Sears discussed the possible involvement of the need for power, the excitement of the hunt and the social pressure on men to be strong and "manly." Sears also noted that the media may play an important role in shaping the serial murderer's behavior. The percentage of current television movies that are based on violence or have very violent content is extremely high and the sensational style in which many newspapers report about murders cannot help but influence behavior, especially for those who may be prone to it in the first place. For example,

when John Gacy killed young boys, he employed the same techniques and choose the same kind of victims that has been described
in newspaper accounts of Dean Corll's serial killings and Sears
suggested that Gacy may have been motivated to kill by hearing
about Corll.

Sears studied the typology of organized nonsocial and disorganized asocial serial murderers (reviewed in Chapter 7) and concluded that it was useful, though he suggested that it was necessary
to include a mixed type so that all serial killers could fit somewhere
in the typology.

The frustration-aggression hypothesis (Dollard et al., 1938) argues that aggression is always a consequence of frustration. Many
murderers—both single and multiple—have lives that are filled
with frustrations stemming from bad childhood experiences. These
include parental abuse and failure to meet the child's basic needs
as well as failure with interpersonal relationships, and problems
with school, employment and the military. Obviously, like other
murderers, serial killers can be angry at someone—a significant
other for example—and they may choose victims who represent
this hated person. For them, killing is a form of displaced aggression. However, it is difficult to fit many of the known serial killers
into this pattern.

Sears discussed Megargee's (1966) typology of overcontrolled
murderers (who suppress their anger until it breaks through in a
tremendously violent act) versus undercontrolled murderers (who
react immediately to anyone who insults or frustrates them). Sears
felt that this typology did not always apply to serial murderers
because they often exhibit both styles of violence. However, it might
be possible to view the serial murderer as an overcontrolled type in
whom the anger builds up quickly (in weeks or months) rather than
slowly (over years).

Sears' major contribution, however, was his discovery of Wertham's
concept of the *catathymic crisis*. Wertham (1937) noted that murder
can be a repetitive action focused on a single idea—namely that the
person must commit a violent act. There is a definite plan together
with the urge to carry it out. This differs from a true obsession. The
catathymic crisis has five stages:

1. An initial thinking disorder which, for the serial murderer,
    centers on his abnormally violent (and sometimes sexually
    aberrant) fantasies.
2. The crystallization of a plan for carrying out acts of violence.

3. Extreme tension culminating in a violent crisis in which the brutal act is acted out.
4. A resulting subsequent period of calmness and the resumption of normalcy.
5. Insight and recovery after the re-establishment of an inner equilibrium.

It is this final stage that the serial murderer fails to reach. Instead, after reaching stage 4, the serial murderer goes back to stage 1. This makes the catathymic crisis *chronic* for the serial killer rather than *acute.*

Wertham felt that this pattern prevents a more serious psychiatric disorder from developing in the individual. If the tension were not relieved by the action, a full-blown psychosis might take shape.

Sears traced the reception given to Wertham's concept. Menninger and Mayman (1956) described a syndrome which they named *episodic dyscontrol,* a syndrome later divided into a primary type where there is little planning or control and a secondary type where there is premeditation and control (Monroe, 1981). In the third edition of their Diagnostic and Statistical Manual (1981), the American Psychiatric Association included a psychiatric disorder which they labeled *explosive personality.* There is an isolated type and an intermittent type, the latter being one in which the explosive episodes are repeated. The revised third edition (1987) removed the isolated type and cautioned that the intermittent type may not be a valid psychiatric disorder. Despite these words of caution, Sears argued that the catathymic crisis described by Wertham (or some variant of it) provides a distinct psychiatric syndrome which fits many serial murderers and, therefore, has merit.

Burgess and Colleagues

Burgess and colleagues (1986) proposed what they have called a motivational model of sexual homicide which they have applied to serial murderers. They noted five main elements in the model.

1. *Ineffective Social Environment.* The murderers in their sample failed to bond to the significant others in their family, such as parents and siblings. Mostly this was the result of the abusive, rejecting or neglectful behavior by their parents or caretakers.
2. *Formative Events.* Traumatic events of murderers' early lives,

such as physical and sexual abuse, shape their developing thought patterns and social life. Their thinking remains fixated on these traumatic events, causing them to feel helpless. As a result, aggressive fantasies emerge that help them achieve in a fantasy life the dominance and control that is absent from their actual lives. These consequences lead to failures in normal development and the inability to form satisfying interpersonal relationships.

3. *Patterned Responses.* In response to these early events, murderers develop primarily negative, unpleasant personality traits, such as a sense of social isolation, preferences for autoerotic activities and hostility. They also develop an antisocial view of the world. The world is hostile and so must be forced to yield gratification regardless of the impact on others.

4. *Actions Toward Others.* Their thoughts, and eventually their actions toward others, are based on domination. Cruelty toward animals and other children during childhood develops into more violent behaviors during adolescence and adulthood.

5. *Feedback Filter.* In his social isolation, the murderer is proud of his violent behaviors and justifies them to himself. With successive assaults, he corrects his mistakes and preserves and refines his fantasies.

In a study that bears a little on these ideas, Prentky and associates (1989) compared 25 serial sexual murderers with 17 single-victim sexual murderers. The serial murderers more often reported fantasies of rape and murder. They also reported a higher incidence of sexually deviant behavior, including fetishism (sexual arousal by inanimate objects) and transvestism (cross-dressing). Incidentally, the serial murderers more often left an organized crime scene (see Chapter 7).

John Money

Money (1990), an expert on these theories, reported the case of a possible serial murderer who had committed at least two "lust murders" (Money did not specify the exact number) and many rapes. Money saw sexual sadism as a "brain disease," meaning that he preferred explanations that focused on genetic, biochemical and physiological factors. Money noted that the area of the brain responsible for sexual behavior, the limbic system, is also responsible for predation and attack. In the sexual sadist, Money hypothesized that messages relating to sexual behavior and attack are transmitted simultaneously, a defect caused by faulty functioning, resulting perhaps from a tumor, an open or closed head injury, or some defect too small to be identified using present-day techniques of brain scanning. Money suggested that the dysfunction was episodic (or paroxysmal) in nature, similar to nonconvulsive types of epilepsy (especially temporal lobe or psychomotor seizures).

Money felt that four other factors could also contribute to the appearance of sexual sadism:

1. Genetic factors, in which case an investigator could find similar behaviors in the relatives of the offender.
2. Abnormalities in hormonal functions, not only in puberty and adulthood when hormones affect sexual and aggressive behavior, but also prenatally when hormonal levels in the mother can have a deleterious effect on the fetus.
3. Child-rearing factors, in particular pathological relationships between children and their parents (and other close relatives), especially if there is physical and sexual abuse of the children. For example, in their discussion of the sexual dynamics of sexually motivated murder, Schlesinger and Revitch (1983) reported that maternal overprotection, seduction, infantilization or outright rejection of the son by the mother was common. Maternal sexual indiscretion and promiscuity also played an important part. Schlesinger and Revitch wondered why the mother's sexual promiscuity was more upsetting to sons than the father's promiscuity was to daughters. In Western societies especially, men need to see their mothers as pure and asexual, and Schlesinger and Revitch suggested that this explained the particularly sadistic victimization of prostitutes.[1]
4. Psychiatric disorder can also play a role, in particular such syndromes as temporal lobe epilepsy, bipolar affective disorder (which used to be known as manic-depressive psychosis), antisocial personality disorder (associated with sociopathic and sometimes psychopathic behavior) and dissociative disorders (disorders which involve amnesia, such as multiple personality).[2]

Note that Money, as a psychologist, ignored the influence of societal and cultural factors such as those noted by Caputi (1987) and Leyton (1989), but obviously such factors should also be included in any list of contributing factors.

Money reported details on a particular defendant whom he had been asked to evaluate.[3] Let us look at each area in turn.

1. *Genetic Factors.* The defendant's father had raped the defendant's mother when she was 15 and threatened to kill her if she did not marry him. The association between sexuality and violence could, therefore, have a genetic basis for the defendant. However, this kind of a man may also have sexually assaulted his wife (and other women) during his marriage and so provided a role model for his son. Thus, his son's sexuality may be learned rather than inherited.[4] Nonetheless, the father's sexual behavior is relevant to the case (as might be the sexual behavior of the defendant's siblings, grandparents, etc.).

2. *Hormonal Factors.* The defendant grew breasts during his teenage years, as did a male cousin, a condition known as gynecomastia. The defendant's breasts were surgically removed when he was 15. He had sparse body hair and his level of circulating testosterone was lower than is typical for a man. On the other hand, gross inspection of his chromosomes and pituitary hormones (the hormones that in turn control the production and secretion of testosterone by the testicles) seemed normal. Although an excess of testosterone might seem more likely to lead to sexual sadism, Money noted that a deficit was not uncommon in sexual offenders.

3. *Child-Rearing Experiences.* Although there was no evidence of sexual abuse of the defendant, he did sleep in his mother's bed until a late age (except when she brought a lover home). This sexually titillating situation is thought to provoke high levels of unconscious and conscious anxiety in children and may result in later violence. For example, Lee Harvey Oswald, the alleged assassin of John F. Kennedy, slept in his mother's bed until he was a teenager (Lester and Lester, 1975).

4. *Psychiatric Disorder.* The defendant had a history of episodic insomnia, agitation and not eating when he had his sexually sadistic fantasies. This may have resulted from a manic-depressive bipolar disorder. However, the defendant did not appear to have dominantly depressive episodes. Patients with bipolar affective disorder usually have depressive episodes,

though a small minority have significant manic episodes. The defendant believed that women liked to be raped, though not killed, and this suggested to Money that the defendant possibly had a schizoid personality disorder. Although the defendant had been a member of a wild gang when he was a teenager, he did not appear to have an antisocial personality disorder. He had no signs of epilepsy. However, he had elements of a multiple personality disorder, for he talked of the two sides of his personality as "Good Bobby" and "Bad Bobby."

5. *Brain Damage.* The defendant had five head injuries between the ages of 3 and 9, one of which (being hit by a car at age 7) required hospitalization. When he was 20, he was thrown from a motorcycle, which left him unconscious. He suffered damage to his left eye and left ear as a result. An electroencephalogram (EEG) revealed possible abnormalities in the patient's limbic system on the left side of the brain. Therefore, the possibility of brain damage existed. After the motorcycle accident, the defendant became hypersexual. According to his wife, his frequency of sexual orgasms (from sexual intercourse and masturbation) went up from nine a week to over 30 a week. His episodes of sexual fantasizing with sadistic content also began at this time. In prison, these episodes were controlled with the medication Sinequan, which suggested to Money a physiological etiology.

We can see, therefore, that an expert asks questions, demands psychological and physiological tests and notes events that a nonexpert would not. Therefore, in published cases of serial murderers by journalists and lay writers, there is often a glaring omission of all kinds of information which is absolutely essential for understanding the possible etiology of the case.

Joel Norris

Norris (1989) presented a profile of the serial killer based on interviews with about a dozen serial murderers and a survey of more than 300 others. Some of the aspects of the profile he presented are simply characteristics of the typical serial murderer, but other aspects have causal implications for the behavior pattern. However, it must be remembered that Norris restricts his consideration to those serial murders that fit the popular image—typically a man who stalks, rapes and murders victims to satisfy sexual and dominance desires. Norris's profile has 21 elements, each of which is discussed below.

Ritualistic Behavior

The ritual of the serial murderer serves to structure his fantasies and actual violence and is used by investigators to recognize that one particular individual is responsible for several murders. Often the ritual seems to be that of an uncivilized and inhuman person, a way of satisfying a primitive, animal-like instinct. Thus, Norris sees the pattern of serial murder as stemming from the subcortical structures of the brain, structures that are prominent in determining animal behavior, but that in humans are supposed to be under the control of the more-developed cortex we possess. The behavior also seems regressive, for the serial murderer often uses parts of the victims or their possessions as "totem objects," much as children cling to their blankets or teddy bears.

Norris believes that the ritual is determined by childhood traumas experienced by the individual and the act of murder becomes a play in which the murderer acts outs these traumas again and again. For example, Norris suggests that Henry Lee Lucas, who claimed to have killed hundreds of people across North America (mostly female hitchhikers who were sexually assaulted before and after their death), was actually killing his mother over and over again.[*]

Masks of Sanity

As others have noted, the serial murderer does not typically appear to be "crazy" in day-to-day life. He has a socially acceptable facade and conforms most of the time to the society in which he lives. For example, while Ted Bundy was killing women students in Seattle, he was studying for a pre-law degree, working in local politics, volunteering at a suicide prevention hotline and had a steady girlfriend.

Norris describes serial murderers in psychiatric terms in a rather confused way. He mentions psychopathic traits (a disorder now called antisocial personality disorder), losses of memory (now called dissociative disorders), multiple personality (one form of dissocia-

---

[*] Lucas' mother was an alcoholic who worked as a prostitute. He murdered her when he was 23 and was imprisoned for the crime (Hickey, 1991).

tive disorder in which the different aspects of the personality do not remember the experiences of one another) and gaps in reality (which is not a precise term). However, Norris claims that 88 percent of serial murderers have one or more psychiatric symptoms, but are not necessarily severely disturbed.

Compulsivity

Serial murderers appear to have compulsive traits in their behavior, not only in their murdering behavior, but also in other aspects of their life, such as concern with their physical appearance, neatness around their home, obsessions with personal hygiene, keeping records of their crimes and preserving parts of their victims or the victims' possessions.

Norris felt that obsessive attention to detail and compulsiveness in the performance of daily and ritual activities were indicative of violence. Norris suggested that this obsessive-compulsiveness provides a cushion against an uncertain world. Angyal (1965) noted that obsessive-compulsive behavior was an effort by the child to cope with an unpredictable world. If parents are inconsistent, then the child cannot predict how they will react. Therefore, children turn to rituals, superstitions and obsessive-compulsive behavior as a magic way to relieve anxiety about the world. "If I do this, then Daddy will be nice to me," or "If I do this in that way, then the day will go well." Norris argued that this pattern does not predict violence in the neurotic person, but it does predict violence in the psychopath.

Search for Help

Several of the serial murderers reviewed by Norris made appeals for help at some point in their criminal careers. They expressed concern about their loss of control, their violent impulses, or their dysfunctional families.

Pathological Liars

Norris suggested that people prone to episodic violence are often pathological liars. Norris saw this as a symptom of psychopathy in the murderers and also as a result of damage to the limbic system of the brain, the hypothalamus or the temporal lobe. This sort of lying can also result from epileptic-like seizures in the brain that could cause partial loss of consciousness and hallucinations.

Suicidal Tendencies

Norris noted that several serial murderers had committed suicide or had a history of suicidal ideation and suicide attempts and he suggested that many serial murderers are chronically suicidal. Some deal with the desire to kill themselves by becoming careless in their killing habits, such as letting a victim escape so that they can be caught and imprisoned.

History of Sexual Assault

Many of the serial murderers had a long history of violence and assaultive behavior, sometimes beginning in childhood with cruelty toward other children.

Deviant Sexual Behavior

Similarly, many of the serial murderers had long histories of deviant sexual behavior, including exhibitionism, bestiality (sex with animals) and incest.

Head Trauma or Other Injuries

Norris noted that many serial murderers had a history of trauma to the head, sometimes as a result of lack of oxygen at birth, sometimes from injuries in childhood and sometimes from accidents in adulthood.

This suggestion by Norris is consistent with theories of murder in general. For example, Palmer (1960) found that ordinary murderers, compared to nonmurderers, were more likely to have had difficult births (including forceps injuries during delivery), congenital and postnatally acquired physical deformities, serious illnesses as children (including epilepsy and pneumonia) and serious accidents. Twenty-six percent of the murderers (versus none of the nonmurderers) fell on their heads as children. Palmer interpreted his findings using the frustration-aggression hypothesis. He argued that the murderers had experienced more physical and psychological frustrations than had their brothers and that this contributed to the appearance of aggression as adults. Norris, however, saw the high incidence of head trauma as increasing the probability of brain damage and the brain damage increased in turn the probability of violent behavior.

One case in point is that of Robert Long, who murdered 10 women in the Tampa Bay area in Florida in 1984. To say the least, Long had an accident-filled past. As a young child, Long fell from a swing, had his eye pierced by a stick and lost consciousness. The next year he fell from his bike. The year after that he was hit by a car and suffered a severe concussion, lost several teeth and was knocked unconscious. He was later thrown from a horse. After Long married and served in the Army, he was almost killed in a motorcycle crash that fractured his skull and left him in a semiconscious state for several weeks. The last accident caused him to have vision problems and severe headaches that persisted for the rest of his life. After he was arrested for the serial murders, an examination revealed brain damage in the left temporal lobe of the cortex. Long still had numbness in his face and a limp as a result of the accident. His violent behavior appeared after this final accident.

History of Chronic Drug and Alcohol Abuse

Many serial murderers have been addicted to drugs, alcohol or both. Often they were intoxicated during the commission of the murders. Robert Long used LSD and marijuana in the years before he began murdering and he drank large quantities of alcohol when he was searching for victims. Carlton Gary, who murdered elderly women in Columbus, Georgia, was a cocaine addict.

Norris, who strongly believed that brain damage facilitates the appearance of the pattern of serial murder, saw drug and alcohol use as increasing the risk of brain damage, particularly to those parts of the brain responsible for the appearance and the inhibition of violent behavior.

Drug and Alcohol Abuse by the Parents

Many serial murderers had parents who abused drugs or alcohol, a feature which leads to a dysfunctional home, increases the risk of abuse of the children and suggests the possibility of an inherited predisposition to drug and alcohol abuse in particular and to psychiatric disorder in general.

Physical and Psychological Abuse

Norris felt that almost all serial murderers were abused as children, both physically and emotionally. At the very least, they experienced separations from one or both parents, but severe physical abuse was also quite common. Norris suggested that abuse by the mother was particularly common, but perhaps this results from the fact that the majority of the serial killers he reported on were men who killed women. Henry Lee Lucas, mentioned earlier in this chapter, was repeatedly beaten by his mother and her pimp, often to the point of losing consciousness. Not only did this abusive childhood leave him with little self-worth, but it left Lucas with a huge reservoir of aggression that he tried to release by abusing objects, animals and other people. His first murder was committed when he was 14 and he murdered his mother when he was 23; neither seemed to help him release his pent-up anger. Ed Kemper, who murdered six female hitchhikers in 1972 and 1973, was so afraid of his mother's voice that, after he murdered her, he severed her head, cut out her vocal cords, burned them and put them down the garbage disposal.

Unwanted Pregnancy

Norris drew attention to an important aspect of the abuse that most murderers suffered—they were unwanted by their parents. Some of the serial murderers in Norris' study were not only unwanted, but were also punished for having been born.

Difficult Pregnancies

Many of the mothers of the serial murderers had a difficult time during pregnancy, sometimes because of drug and alcohol abuse, sometimes because of extreme poverty and lack of medical care and sometimes simply because the mother did not want to be pregnant. Again, though Norris gave this feature a separate place in his listing, it can also be seen as another factor that increases the risk of physical and emotional abuse to the child after birth. Norris also saw drug and alcohol abuse and lack of good medical care as increasing the risk of fetal and perinatal brain damage.

Unhappy Childhoods

Norris noted that almost none of the serial murderers in his study had happy childhoods and few of them were able to feel pleasure as adults.

Cruelty to Animals

Norris noted that as children, many of the serial murderers he studied were cruel to animals. Henry Lee Lucas tortured animals until they died and then had sex with their remains. Robert Long abused his mother's pet dog out of jealousy. It has been noted that three traits in children appear to predict later violence: cruelty to animals and children, firesetting and bedwetting (Hellman and Blackman, 1966; Heller et al., 1984). This triad of symptoms seems to imply a strong level of frustration-aggression and a problem with impulse control.

Firesetting Tendencies

Norris seemed to be aware of a firesetting tendency in serial murderers since he noted that some of his subjects showed an early interest in setting fires; he gave Carlton Gary and Henry Lee Lucas as examples.

Neurological Impairment

Because Norris was convinced that brain damage played a role in the development of the serial murderer, he should really have listed the possibility of neurological impairment first. Norris noted that almost all serial murderers show signs of neurological impairment, both hard and soft signs.[*] Norris listed the following signs as predictive of neurological impairment: dyslexia, reading, mathematical and directional problems; hypergraphia; grandiosity; hypervigilance; hyper- and hyposexuality; hyperreligiosity; visual or auditory hallucinations; loose, rambling, illogical thought processes; feelings of persecution; chronic feelings of isolation, alienation or withdrawal; prolonged crying spells and chronic depression; incontinence; sleep disorders; difficulties with spatial coordination and perception; poor muscular coordination; seizures or seizure-like episodes; reading or mathematical disabilities resistant to remediation; chronic or migraine headaches; lability of moods; and choreiform or animal-like body movements.

Some of the items in Norris's list are of dubious relevance to neurological impairment. Depression, for example, is a symptom of affective disorders (depressive or manic-depressive disorders, now called unipolar and bipolar affective disorders), while hallucinations are a symptom of schizophrenia. Some of the items are similar,

---

[*] Hard signs are convincing evidence of brain damage, while soft signs are hints that brain malfunction may exist.

if not identical, such as reading, mathematical and directional problems and reading or mathematical disabilities resistant to re-mediation. However, the general drift is important, namely that neurological impairment is predictive of later violence.

Norris focuses especially on the possibility that a brain syndrome such as psychomotor epilepsy characterizes serial murderers, and that neurological dysfunction to the limbic system and the temporal lobe and possible damage to the hypothalamus can very possibly affect the hormonal balance in the body.

Genetic Disorders

Norris suggested that the presence of congenital physical abnormalities suggests genetic abnormalities in the brain. Norris argued that, since the brain develops in the fetus at the same time as the anatomy, particularly the skin, abnormalities in the skin and cartilage are associated with abnormalities in the brain, but he does not give any scientific references for this assertion. Norris suggested that the presence of three to five of the following features is predictive of brain damage: bulbous fingertips, fine or "electric" hair that will not stay combed, hair whorls, an abnormal head circumference, upper or lower eyelids that join the nose (epicanthus), abnormally larger or smaller distance between the tear ducts of the eyes (hyperteliorism), low-seated ears, earlobes which extend upward and backward toward the crown of the head, malformed ears, asymmetrical ears, very soft or pliable ears, high-steepled palate, roof of mouth steepled or flat and narrow, forward tongue with deep ridges, speckled tongue with smooth or rough spots, curved fifth finger, a singular transverse palmar crease, third toe longer or equal in length to second toe, partial syndactyly of two middle toes, larger than normal gap between first and second toes, abnormalities in teeth and abnormalities in dermatoglyphics (fingerprints).

Biochemical Symptoms

Norris believed that toxic poisoning was common in serial murderers, either generated internally or from high levels of toxins in the environment. This toxic poisoning could be caused by chronic malnutrition or substance abuse. Norris also hypothesized that serial murderers have hormonal cycles, much like menstrual cycles, in which the hormones that govern fear and violence are generated in a rhythm regulated by the hypothalamus. These hormonal imbalances can be indicated indirectly by abnormal sleep patterns or directly by measurements of hormonal levels.

Norris reported a study by William Walsh who tested 10 serial murderers for the chemical composition of their hair as a way of ascertaining chemical imbalances in their bodies. Nine of the 10 had low levels of copper and high levels of sodium and potassium and very high levels of lead and cadmium in their hair, a pattern that is common in violent psychopaths.

Feelings of Powerlessness or Inadequacy

Norris held that feelings of powerlessness and inadequacy lie behind the child's development of antisocial patterns of behavior, particularly toward those weaker than himself.

Comment

The foregoing elements may be moving us in a direction different from that which Norris intended. Norris saw the profile he presented as defining a new syndrome, hitherto ignored by psychiatrists and criminologists. However, what Norris has actually accomplished is to make the serial murderer seem quite similar in many ways to the average murderer. For example, childhood experiences of abuse, possible brain damage and a history of drug and alcohol abuse have been hypothesized by some to characterize the backgrounds of murderers in general. Norris has presented elements of a conventional neuroscience perspective on violence and the frustration-aggression theory as basic to an understanding of the serial murderer and most of the major authorities he quotes in his book were discussing the average murderer rather than serial murderers.[*]

However, Norris' work is provocative because he presents a detailed profile for the serial murderer that could serve as the basis for a research project. The profile also has elements from a variety of sources (physiological, psychological and social) and from childhood. This permits a test of the usefulness of these and other elements in predicting later serial violence.[5]

---

[*] Marvin Wolfgang and Dorothy Lewis are two examples. Norris does not provide references to the works of these authorities, but rather relies on interviews that he conducted with them.

The Role of Early Trauma

Although severe trauma in early childhood is often proposed as an important factor in the development of serial killers, very little research has been conducted on this issue. A large amount of research has shown the importance of early physical and sexual abuse in the childhoods of both murderers (Palmer, 1960) and those who commit suicide (Lester, 1992).

Ressler and co-workers (1986) conducted a study that explored the role of childhood sexual abuse in the behavior of serial murderers. In a sample of 28 sexually motivated murderers, many of whom were serial murderers, they found that 43 percent reported being sexually abused before the age of 9 and 32 percent between the ages of 13 and 18. Those sexually abused in childhood were more likely to report the following behavior in childhood: cruelty to animals, isolation, convulsions, cruelty to other children and assaultiveness toward adults. As adolescents they reported more sleep problems, isolation, incidents of running away, self-mutilation, temper tantrums, rebelliousness and assaultiveness toward adults. They were more likely to report sexual conflicts, sexual dysfunction and sexual incompetence as adults and they were also more likely to report deviant sexual practices, including sexual contact with animals, bondage sex, fetishism, obscene telephone calls, indecent exposure (exhibitionism) and cross-dressing. They began to have fantasies of rape at an earlier age than murderers who were not sexually abused and they were more likely to report an aversion to sex both in adolescence and adulthood. Sexually abused murderers were more likely to mutilate the sexual parts of their victims after the murder (for example, the breasts, genitals and abdomen).

The Role of Neutralization

Several criminological theories focus on the way in which criminals rationalize guilt feelings so that they can be free to break the rules of society (Sykes and Matza, 1957). Levi (1981) applied these ideas to the way in which a professional "hit man" comes to feel comfortable with his "career."

Some cultures permit special organizations to kill and special circumstances in which one may kill without feeling guilty, such as soldiers during war or police officers in the line of duty. Subcultures of the society (Wolfgang and Ferracuti, 1969), organizations such as the Mafia (Maas, 1968) and gangs (Yablonsky, 1962) also provide social support for deviant behavior in the members by developing norms to justify the behaviors that are seen as deviant by the rest of society. The killer for an organization such as the Mafia can explain his acts by claiming that he was working for a higher loyalty. The victim can be viewed as an enemy of the organization.

But some professional hit men work alone and so do not have the group and peer support to justify their career choice. How then do such people overcome their inhibitions and avoid serious damage to their self-image? Levi interviewed a free-lance hit man and based his observations on the following case.

The professional hit man has a contract to kill someone whom he typically does not know. The hit man also typically does not know the person hiring him, for the arrangement is usually made by telephone. This arrangement, anonymous in all respects, helps the killer deny his personal role in the killing by keeping the employer anonymous.

After the contract is arranged, a failure to carry out the killing could have dire consequences for the hit man; if he is caught by the law, it could mean the death penalty. Thus, the hit man may see himself as having to go through with the killing as a form of self-defense! Reputation is important for the professional hit man. This reputation depends in large part on how much he was paid for his last hit and how much he can command for the next. To the hit man, killing can then become conceptualized as a "business" or as "just a job." If the person or group did not hire him, then they would hire someone else. This way of thinking greatly facilitates the denial of any wrongdoing. The hit man must also develop his skill—his ability to kill cleanly and efficiently. This focus on technique also directs focus away from the victim.

Levi noted that these neutralization techniques would work well for the experienced hit man, but they would not work as well for the novice, who commands low pay and has relatively poor skills. Thus, the first "kill" is usually upsetting for the hit man. Levi's subject reported being upset when his victim looked at him with an innocent expression that seemed to ask "Why me?" Levi noted that successful prostitutes remain detached from the sexual act and from their clients in the same way that surgeons seek to remain detached, for example, by totally covering the patient on the operating table with a sheet except for the area of incision. Levi's hit man soon failed to notice the target's facial expression, a tactic that facilitated the coldness associated with the professional killer. This coldness is not necessarily a result of the hit man's personality, but a consequence of his neutralization techniques.

Comment

It is clear from this review of theories of serial murder that the theories proposed are identical to those that have been proposed for murder in general. The possibility of brain damage, the role of frustration—especially during childhood—and the impact of society and subculture are each major theories of single-victim murder. Thus, future research on the serial murderer must move toward identifying which variables (or combination of variables) distinguish the serial murderer from the single-victim murderer. No such research has yet appeared and thus the theories reviewed in this chapter have not yet been adequately tested.

Notes

1. Schlesinger and Revitch noted that a general hostility toward women was more common in adult murderers, whereas incestuous desires and maternal sexual conduct are more salient for adolescent murderers.

2. Schlesinger and Revitch (1983) saw the acts of sexually motivated murderers as compulsive offenses motivated by inner conflicts.

3. Money did not identify the murderer, but the details of the case fit those of Robert Long (Norris, 1989).

4. Studies of family trees are common in evaluations of clients with both medical and psychiatric problems. A physician often wants to know what diseases a patient's parents and grandparents suffered from and a psychiatrist may be interested in their psychiatric disorders. However, this information rarely "proves" a genetic cause for psychiatric disorders. Disturbed parents may pass on defective genes to their children, but they also tend to produce pathological environments in which their children are raised. Thus, we cannot distinguish between the inherited factors and the learning experiences.

5. Schlesinger and Revitch (1983) suggested a shorter list of predictive signs for sexually motivated murder: (1) a history of unprovoked attacks on and mistreatment of women; (2) crimes of breaking and entering committed alone and under bizarre circumstances; (3) fetishism of female underclothing and destruction of female clothes; (4) expression of hatred, contempt or fear of women; (5) violence against animals, particularly cats; (6) violent fantasies; (7) confusion of sexual identity which may be noticeable on projective psychological tests; (8) sexual inhibitions and preoccupation with sexual morality; and (9) feelings of isolation and blurring of reality boundaries.

References

Angyal, A. *Neurosis and Treatment*. New York: Wiley, 1965.

Brickman, J. Female lives, feminist deaths. *Canadian Psychology* 33:128-143, 1992.

Brittain, R.P. The sadistic murderer. *Medicine, Science and the Law* 10:199-207, 1970.

Burgess, A.W., C.R. Hartman, R.K. Ressler, J.E. Douglas and A. McCormack. Sexual homicide. *Journal of Interpersonal Violence* 1: 251-272, 1986.

Caputi, J. *The Age of Sex Crime*. Bowling Green, OH: Bowling Green State University Press, 1987.

Dollard, J., L. Doob, N. Miller, O.H. Mowrer and R. Sears. *Frustration and Aggression*. New Haven, CT: Yale University Press, 1938.

Heller, M.A., S.M. Ehrlich and D. Lester. Childhood cruelty to animals, firesetting and enuresis as correlates of competence to stand trial. *Journal of General Psychology* 110:151-153, 1984.

Hellman, D.S. and N. Blackman. Enuresis, firesetting and cruelty to animals. *American Journal of Psychiatry* 122:431-1435, 1966.

Hickey, E.W. *Serial Murderers and Their Victims*. Pacific Grove, CA: Brooks/Cole, 1991.

Holmes, R.M. and J. De Burger. *Serial Murder*. Beverly Hills, CA: Sage, 1988.

Krafft-Ebing, R. von. *Psychopathia Sexualis*. Philadelphia: F.A. Davis, 1892.

Lester, D. *Why People Kill Themselves*. Springfield, IL: Charles C Thomas, 1992.

Lester, D. and G. Lester. *Crime of Passion*. Chicago: Nelson-Hall, 1975.

Levi, K. Becoming a hit man. *Urban Life* 10:47-63, 1981.

Leyton, E. *Compulsive Killers*. New York: New York University Press, 1986.

Leyton, E. *Hunting Humans*. London: Penguin, 1989.

Lunde, D. *Murder and Madness*. New York: Norton, 1979

Maas, P. *The Valachi Papers*. New York: Putnam, 1968.

Megargee, E.I. Undercontrolled and overcontrolled personality types in extreme antisocial aggression. *Psychological Monographs* 80(3):611, 1966.

Menninger, K. and M. Mayman. Episodic dyscontrol. *Bulletin of the Menninger Clinic* 20:153-165, 1956.

Money, J. Forensic sexology. *American Journal of Psychotherapy*, 44:26-36, 1990.

Monroe, R.A. The problem of impulsivity in personality disturbances. In J.R. Lion (ed.) *Personality Disorders*. Baltimore: Williams and Wilkins, 1981.

Norris, J. *Serial Killers*. New York: Anchor, 1989.

Palmer, S. *A Study of Murder*. New York: Crowell, 1960.

Prentky, R.A., A.W. Burgess, F. Rokous, A. Lee, C. Hartman, R. Ressler and J. Douglas. The presumptive role of fantasy in serial sexual homicide. *American Journal of Psychiatry* 146:887-891, 1989.

Ressler, R.K., A.W. Burgess, C.R. Hartman, J.E. Douglas and A. McCormack. Murderers who rape and mutilate. *Journal of Interpersonal Violence* 1:273-287, 1986.

Schlesinger, L.B. and E. Revitch. Sexual dynamics in homicide and assault. In L.B. Schlesinger and E. Revitch (eds.) *Sexual Dynamics of Anti-Social Behavior.* Springfield, IL: Charles C Thomas, 1983.

Sears, D. *To Kill Again.* Wilmington, DE: Scholarly Resources, 1991.

Sykes, G.M. and D. Matza. Techniques of neutralization. *American Journal of Sociology* 22:664-670, 1957.

Wertham, F. The catathymic crisis. *Archives of Neurology and Psychiatry* 37:974-978, 1937.

Toch, H. *Violent Men.* Chicago: Aldine, 1969.

Wolfgang, M.E. and F. Ferracuti. The *Subculture of Violence.* New York: Tavistock, 1969.

Yablonsky, L. *The Violent Gang.* New York: Macmillan, 1962.

Chapter 9

The System Response

There are two social systems that are employed when responding to serial murder: (1) the criminal justice system which must identify, catch and incarcerate the offender and (2) the mental health system which helps survivors. Survivors are either people who have lost a loved one to death (in this case, due to serial murder), or those who have been present during a murderer's killing spree and were able to escape as well. Even though the term survivor does not fit very well to people who experience high levels of anxiety as a result of having a serial murderer do his "work" in their community, it is sometimes applied to them.

The Criminal Justice System

The criminal justice system has had great difficulty dealing with serial murder. In the first part of this century, American police departments were not well equipped to track down local serial murderers because knowledge about murderers in general was limited and investigatory techniques were crude. Because the majority of serial murderers kill victims in several locales, even the simple determination that a serial murderer is at work requires cooperation between police departments—sometimes between different cities and states. In fact, cooperation between departments is a problem that the law enforcement community is still grappling with. It is more than probable that in the past, many serial murderers were not identified and this is still true today, although not to the extent that it used to be. This problem makes invalid most comparisons of the current frequency of serial murder with its frequency in the past and this is also the case with the comparisons from country to country.

Furthermore, there are currently over 20,000 law enforcement agencies in America! This fragmentation of police departments also invalidates the comparison of the frequency of serial murder in America with other countries, because other countries often have uniform and centralized law enforcement agencies.

Egger (1984) noted that about 66 percent of contemporary murderers are in custody within 14 hours of the crime they committed. If murders are not solved within 48 hours, the likelihood of solving the crime drops markedly. The clearance rate for murder (that is, the percentage of murders that are solved) dropped from 93 percent in 1962 to 74 percent in 1982. Egger suggested that this drop is the result of an increasing percentage of stranger-to-stranger murders in which motives are often obscure, thereby making it more difficult for police to solve cases.

Egger noted that many serial murder cases were solved by luck or because the serial murderer became careless or decided that he wanted to be caught. For example, after killing 10 women in 1984 in the Tampa Bay area, Robert Long choose to let one victim get away after he sexually assaulted her for 26 hours. She immediately went to the police with her story and the evidence she provided allowed the police to find and arrest Long.

Cooperative Programs

One way to improve the detection and capture of serial murderers is by increasing the cooperation between law enforcement agencies in different cities and states. Steps in this direction were taken by the FBI when they set up the National Center for the Analysis of Violent Crime in 1984. The Center has four programs: a research and development program to acquire knowledge about serial murder, a training program for members of the criminal justice community, a profiling and consultation program to provide profiles of the serial murderer prepared by experts and the Violent Criminal Apprehension Program (VICAP).

The VICAP tries to match cases nationally that could be linked to the same individual (Green and Whitmore, 1993). It is a national clearinghouse that collects, reviews and analyzes reports submitted by all of the different law enforcement agencies in the country. An effective program of this sort must include the following components:

1. A nationally networked, central computer site. Everyone even remotely involved with serial killers (police officers and police departments, investigators, forensic pathologists, government officers, private detectives, medical examiners, lawyers, special agencies, etc.) should provide any information they may have about murderers and victims for input into this program. This large database of information on both suspects and victims can be output in many different ways to produce any type of report needed. Experts at the central site produce reports when they are requested or when important themes are recognized.

2. A group that inputs all information into the main system. This group should be able to provide every police department and every law enforcment agency (as well as the many others who can benefit from such information) in every state with up-to-the-minute information on murderers and victims of murderers.

3. All murder cases and all victims suspected of death by murder should be examined in a standardized way and in a routine format by all police officers and departments as well as all of the other different groups involved to those who input to the main computer. Local police should have a list of necessary information that they should try to obtain and it must be standardized.

4. All evidence collected in a case should be placed in an exact location at all times (and logged in the computer) to prevent items from being lost.

5. Written collaborative agreements between the many, many different law enforcement agencies in the country should be drawn up, so that each department will agree to provide the main source with all the information they have. It has been hard to get cooperation from local police departments.

Green and Whitmore gave several examples of work conducted early on by the VICAP. In one case, 14 agencies in the Midwest had collected data on 26 murders of young white males, all of whom were believed to be homosexual. A meeting of all of those involved led to the realization that 10 of the murders had probably been committed by one murderer. Eight of the cases were grouped together as the work of a possible second serial murderer and three cases could possibly have been the work of a third murderer. That left five cases with no apparent similarities to each another or to the other three already identified groups. The meeting also led to identification of nine possible suspects.

In a second case, a captured serial murderer admitted that he had committed six murders on the West Coast. The man was a truck driver and because of this he drove all over the country. The VICAP facilitated tracking the murderer's route and were able to place him at different times in 37 states. A meeting was arranged of law enforcement representatives in four of these states. Critical evidence was identified as a result of this meeting. For example, the murderer had a locker in one of the states, the contents of which the local law enforcement agency was just about to turn over to the murderer's family. Instead, the contents of the locker were seized as important evidence. The murderer was planning on plea bargaining, but the prosecutors who were at the meeting agreed that they would not let him do this and thereby avoid the death penalty.

The Mental Health System

Help for Victims

Victims or survivors of any catastrophe or acute crisis can be helped by a mental health team. Creamer and associates (1991) noted that victims of catastrophes require six elements:

1. Victims need to be provided with truthful information about the incident they were involved in, such as what happened, what has happened since and all other pertinent information. It is especially important to identify any rumors that may have come up and replace them with accurate information. Information permits victims to begin to achieve some sort of closure.
2. They need to be educated about how trauma usually affects people. One of the things they will learn from this is that their emotional reactions are not necessarily abnormal and that they are not "crazy."
3. It is often helpful for victims to confront the traumatic memories of the event. Facilitation of cognitive, behavioral and emotional re-encounters with the event can speed the recovery process.
4. Social support networks are helpful in the recovery of victims. Development and utilization of such networks must be encouraged.

5. Victims often feel that they have lost control. Helping victims take an active part in decision-making helps them re-establish a sense of control.
6. Trained mental health professionals must be available to counsel those who need more intensive therapeutic work.

Case Example: A Mass Murder in Australia

Creamer and his co-workers illustrated their suggestions by examining a mass murder that took place on December 8, 1987, in an office building in Melbourne, Australia, where a lone gunman shot and killed eight people and injured several others before he jumped out a window and died when he hit the sidewalk.

The initial response by the police to the incident was delayed because they thought that it may have been a hostage situation. Time passed before the building was declared safe and before medics were permitted inside to attend to the injured. Although many of the 800 employees managed to leave the building, some barricaded themselves in their offices. Others had to deal with their dead and wounded colleagues without any professional assistance.

To ensure that the assistance program was not seen by survivors as having been imposed from the outside, a task force was set up with senior management and staff representatives. The team consulted with staff and management constantly during the course of the following year to make sure that the program was being accepted by everyone.

For this case, a mental health professional was assigned to oversee the recovery program, to consult with the management and to facilitate the provision of group and individual counseling. Counseling staff were obtained from local mental health agencies and crisis intervention volunteer groups.

A "recovery center" was immediately set up in the building as a place where employees could obtain information, meet with colleagues to discuss the incident and to have easy access to counselors. The employees who had not returned to work within two days of the murders were contacted by staff from the recovery center to see if they were okay and, if necessary, a counselor was sent to their home to talk to them and to help them return to work. The floors on which people had died were closed off; however, counselors did accompany workers who wished to revisit the places where their friends had died. Counselors also circulated throughout the building, talking to workers and making themselves available to anyone who wanted help.

In addition, three days after the incident, every worker in the building participated in a debriefing session in which educational material about posttraumatic reactions was presented, some discussion of reactions to the incident encouraged and social support networks identified and developed.

After two weeks, the external assistance was withdrawn. A newsletter was created for the building's employees that provided them with information, continued the process of victim and recovery education and gave employees an opportunity to express their opinions and feelings that resulted from the incident. An evening event was organized at which family members of employees could discuss their concerns and reactions to the murders.

Nine months later, a public inquiry was made into the investigation of this mass murder. The team helped prepare the employees who were going to testify and all of the company's employees were helped in advance to deal with media publicity surrounding the incident. Debriefing and personal support services were also offered at that time to any employee who wanted them.

After a year, the services that had been provided began to wind down and the internal organization took over the task of referring employees to outside agencies for help when needed. A memorial service was held on the anniversary of the incident and a stained glass window was commissioned to honor the dead.

The fact that the incident occurred in the work place facilitated the recovery program in that there was a centralized place from which services could be provided. Support networks—made up of fellow employees (which was especially important because some family members grew tired of discussing the events) were readily available.

The incident also had an impact on the larger community in that it increased apprehensiveness about crime. For example, there were pleas made for tighter gun control laws. It was difficult to devise ways of helping members of the general community except by printing articles in the local newspapers and airing segments on television about the psychological effects of trauma and listing the social services that were available.

The response to another mass murder, this time at an advertising agency, was described by Freed and Gandell (1978). Three people were killed and two wounded before the killer, an employee of the firm, committed suicide. A group meeting was held for the staff and

11 of the 75 employees went through psychotherapy for the subsequent year, at the firm's expense.

North and associates (1989) interviewed employees who worked at four different businesses in Arkansas in December 1987 and who were the targets of a shooting spree by a man who had murdered 14 members of his family at home, then went and killed two employees and wounded four others who worked for these firms. Those who actually witnessed the shootings reported having more symptoms of posttraumatic stress disorder than those who were not at work during the shootings. The most common symptoms reported were jumpiness and insomnia. Ninety-one percent of the witnesses turned to friends and relatives for support and 64 percent took advantage of the counseling offered by the firms, compared to 71 percent and 29 percent of the non-present workers, respectively. None of the workers who had a history of psychiatric disorder experienced a recurrence of this disorder.

Help for Indirect Victims

Evidently, even if people are not directly involved in a mass murder, they may still experience psychological effects. Hough and co-workers (1990) interviewed female Mexican-American immigrants, aged 35 to 50, six months after the 1984 massacre at the McDonald's in San Ysidro, California, in which James Huberty killed 21 people and injured 15 others. About one-third of the women who witnessed the shootings reported being upset by the event, 6 percent had severe posttraumatic stress syndrome and another 6 percent reported mild posttraumatic stress syndrome. This syndrome was more common in women who were poor, unemployed, in poor health and not married. As one respondent said:

> I remember those happy children playing in the street and my child plays with them and I think of their mothers and realize it could have been my child. I feel very bad for those children who were killed. It was only an act of God that mine didn't go that day (Hough et al., 1990, p. 85).

Very little work has been done on the trauma felt by direct and indirect victims of serial murderers, partly because the murders are typically spread out over a long period of time and partly because those traumatized by the murders are often scattered, sometimes within a community and sometimes across a country. However, some attention has been given to the trauma caused by serial killers. For example, Spencer and associates (1988) noted that during the abduction and murder of young black males in Atlanta, the city's young black male population experienced a great deal of anxiety. For example, one boy reported: "I was so scared. I couldn't help it. I stayed in the house all the time...I was scared to look at the news on TV" (p. 124). However, a gross comparison of clinical symptoms indicated that children in Atlanta showed no more symptoms than children in four other major cities that did not have a serial murderer on the prowl (Spencer, 1986).

Braddock (1982) also noted an increase in symptoms of distress in the children of Atlanta during the serial murders, including nightmares, bedwetting, dependency, irritability, fear of strangers and going outside. Some children began carrying weapons to school. One boy refused to sleep in his bed because it was near the window and he feared that the killer could see him from the street and might kidnap him. Another boy had just eaten chicken before a newscast about the murders and envisioned the murderer eating children just as he had eaten the chicken. The boy had terrible nightmares of being eaten for the next two nights.

Braddock, who worked for the county, organized training groups for children and parents in any settings he could find: low-income housing areas, community centers, churches, civic groups, places of employment, schools, recreation centers, parks, restaurants and even on street corners. He avoided describing the work as "mental health" and tried to suggest ways that the adults and children could cope with the crisis. He educated parents about the symptoms of fear and stress in children and helped both parents and children develop networks for social support and how to be safe in the streets.

Greaves and co-workers (1982) described a program also designed to help the citizens of Atlanta cope with their fears about the murders that occurred from the summer of 1979 to the spring of 1981, 28 (and possibly 29) children and youths were murdered. As fear in the community rose, the Director of Public Safety appointed a Mental Health Task Force. They organized training programs for health professionals so they could help the children deal with trauma. They developed educational radio and television segments on the emotional and behavioral issues that develop from prolonged anxiety and advised children how to avoid danger (for example, staying off the streets unless they were in groups). Funds were solicited for summer camps and out-of-town visits to relatives were recommended for the children. However, what is most note-

worthy in the report by Greaves is that the mental health professionals involved were anxious to contribute but had little idea of what
they could do.

Those involved in the investigation of multiple murders are also
subject to great trauma, particularly the police (Sewell, 1993). For
example, some of the police officers called to the scene of the 1984
McDonald's massacre in San Ysidro, California had served in Vietnam and they found the sight of the dead and wounded at McDonald's
at least as bad as anything they witnessed in Southeast Asia. What
made the trauma worse for certain police was that their children ate
in that same restaurant and wore the same clothes as some of the
victims. After Ted Bundy had slaughtered two women and attacked
others at the Chi Omega sorority house at Florida State University
in 1978, the scene reminded one investigator of a feeding frenzy by
sharks. Sewell said that posttraumatic stress syndrome is not uncommon in police officers and investigators who are witness to the
aftermath of such crime scenes.

Comment

It is evident that the responses of the criminal justice and mental
health systems to the problem of serial murder are in a preliminary
stage. It is far easier, for example, for mental health professionals to
respond to the survivors of a mass murder incident than to those
distressed by a serial murderer. However, the series of child murders
in Atlanta did stimulate the development of action by mental health
professionals there and more thought needs to be given as to how
the lessons learned in Atlanta can be applied in other settings.

References

Braddock, H.O. Children and stress. *Journal of Non-White Concerns in Personnel and Guidance* 11(1):24-32, 1982.

Brooks, P.R., M.J. Devine, T.J. Green, B.L. Hart and M.D. Moore. Serial
murder. *Police Chief* 54(6):40-44, 1987.

Creamer, M., W.J. Buckingham and P.M. Burgess. A community-based
mental health response to a multiple shooting. *Australian Psychologist*
26:99-102, 1991.

Egger, S.A. A working definition of serial murder and the reduction of
linkage blindness. *Journal of Police Science and Administration* 12:348-357,
1984.

Freed, H.M. and R. Gandell. Murder on the job. *Mental Health and Society*
5:231-240, 1978.

Greaves, G.B., J.S. Currie and A.C. Carter. Atlanta, psychology and the second siege. *American Psychologist* 37:559-568, 1982.

Green, T.J. and J.E. Whitmore. VICAP's role in multiagency serial murder investigations. *Police Chief* 60(6):38-45, 1993.

Hough, R.L., W. Vega, R. Valle, B. Kolody, R.G. del Castillo and H. Tarke. Mental health consequences of the San Ysidro McDonald's massacre. *Journal of Traumatic Stress* 3:71-92, 1990.

North, C.S., E.M. Smith, R.E. McCool and J.M. Shea. Short-term psychopathology in eyewitness to mass murder. *Hospital and Community Psychiatry* 40:1293-1295, 1989.

Sewell, J.D. Traumatic stress of multiple murder investigation. *Journal of Traumatic Stress* 6:103-118, 1993.

Spencer, M.B. Risk and resilience. *Journal of Social Science* 71(1):22-26, 1986.

Spencer, M.B., B. Dobbs and D.P. Swanson. African American adolescents. *Journal of Adolescence* 11:117-137, 1988.

PART II

CASE HISTORIES

Chapter 10

Gilles de Rais: A Serial Murderer of the Fifteenth Century

Gilles de Rais was born in the early 1400s, at a time when the French central government had collapsed and the King of France, Charles VI, was insane. Under the influence of the Hundred Years' War, the country had split into semi-independent fiefdoms. Nobles lived on their private estates, raised their own armies and pursued their own interests—which were primarily the increase of their own wealth. War had devastated the countryside, the Black Death had killed nearly one third of the population in Europe and famine was widespread. Even the Church was in turmoil; there were two Popes, one in Rome and the other in Avignon, and each was backed by rival European nations. The French nobility was being vanquished on the battlefield by common English soldiers and were unable to learn how to change their style of fighting. At Agincourt in 1415, France lost a major battle to King Henry V of England.

Gilles de Rais was the product of a power struggle in France. His father, Guy de Laval, and his mother, Marie de Craon, were distant cousins who were forced to marry in order to pool their combined wealth and keep it in the family. Jeanne la Sage was the last of the Rais family and had no children. To protect the Rais property from the Duke of Brittany, she decided that her second cousin, Guy de Laval, would be her heir if he would adopt the Rais name. But then she changed her mind and chose a more distant relative whose son was Jean de Craon. Both heirs brought suit to the Parlement of Paris and a compromise was achieved. Jean de Craon's daughter would marry Guy de Laval, thus uniting the two disputants. They married in 1404 and the future heir, Gilles de Rais, was born before the end of the year.

Like all aristocratic European children, Gilles was given to a wet nurse who seems to have been affectionate. As he grew up, Gilles became close to his wet nurse's son, his *frère de lait*, and eventually appointed him as his personal chaplain. Gilles' parents most likely had little time for their son. This was common enough in those days; their time was consumed with the duties and the rituals of noble life. As the heir apparent, Gilles was groomed for his future role, surrounded in luxury and given every possible privilege. Thus, like most sons of noble families, Gilles was very spoiled. He had private tutors who attended to his military training and his intellectual education and he did well in these studies.

His younger brother, René, was born in 1407. The two brothers were never close and perhaps even hated each other. In 1415, when Gilles was 10 years old, both of his parents died. His father was gored by a boar while hunting and his mother is thought to have died shortly before him, but because her death records are missing, we are not sure how. Although Gilles was not close with his parents in a modern sense, they were the center of his universe and provided him with security and stability. Their death had a great impact on him. In the same year, Jean de Craon's son and heir was killed in the battle of Agincourt, leaving Gilles the heir of the Craon fortune and motivating Jean to take over the boy's education.

Gilles' first experience of battle was in a dispute in 1420 between the Duke of Brittany and a neighboring family, the Penthièvres. He distinguished himself well on the Duke's behalf. After this, Gilles' grandfather turned to the task of marrying the boy suitably and he chose Catherine de Thouars, a distant cousin of Gilles, whose father owned neighboring estates. There were many rivals for her hand, so Jean de Craon kidnapped her and betrothed her to Gilles. The family and the Church were outraged, but after negotiations, a formal marriage took place in June 1422. Craon's wife died at this time and he married Catherine's grandmother. Gilles' brother René also married into the family, thereby cementing the merger. Not only did Gilles not love Catherine, but he was not in the least bit interested in her and never cared for her. It was a marriage made solely for political purposes.

In 1420, Gilles came of age. He was overbearing, bullying and brutal, and a complete egotist. And he had total control of the Rais fortunes. Benedetti characterizes Gilles' taking control as a child who demanded his toys rather than as an adult who showed a mature desire for responsibility.

Gilles and Joan of Arc

In 1425, Charles VII of France prepared for a renewal of the Hundred Years War. In 1427, Jean de Craon was appointed Lieutenant of Anjou and Gilles organized five companies of troops. Gilles set off for battle with the guidance of an experienced soldier named Guillaume de la Jumellière. He distinguished himself well. After taking the English stronghold at Lude, Gilles arrived at the French court in a blaze of glory.

The King's trusted advisor, Georges de la Trémoille, was Gilles' cousin and this easily facilitated Gilles' quick rise to prominence. In 1428, the English laid siege to Orléans and initial attempts to relieve the city failed. Then, Joan the Maid appeared, promising to raise the siege and to have the Dauphin crowned in Reims cathedral. Gilles was placed in charge of the army that was sent to Orléans with Joan. Joan made several poor military decisions and each time was rescued by Gilles and his forces. Gilles and Joan became firm allies and Gilles himself was won over by her views and tactics. Eventually, in May 1429, the English abandoned the siege and Gilles was made Marshal of France at the early age of 25, an honor that further swelled the family fortune. However, after an abortive attack on Paris, the new King of France decided to consolidate his position and end the campaigns. Joan was no longer needed and Gilles was expected to retire to his estates.

For the next couple of years, Gilles took part in a few small military engagements and a little banditry, robbing travelers and holding others for ransom. His daughter was born in 1429. In 1432, Gilles won his last battle at Lagny, his grandfather, Jean de Craon, died, and Gilles murdered a child—the first of more than one hundred.

The Murders

Hostilities paused in 1433 and at this point, Gilles' life changed dramatically. He had no war to fight and no activities to assuage his lust for torture and killing— a lifestyle that he had become accustomed to and apparently liked. Benedetti (1972) notes that Gilles had been trained to kill, was good at it, and was honored for it.

Perhaps, as a youngster, he developed psychopathic tendencies that allowed him to turn into the monster he became and war only added to the recipe by providing him with a socially acceptable outlet for his desires of brutality. And, perhaps what had been so alluring to Gilles about war was not so much the booty he claimed, but the blood he shed.

Gilles is best conceptualized as a combination of a retired war veteran who enjoyed the brutality of war and a pampered aristocrat who was used to having his pleasures satisfied no matter what the cost to others—and the cost to others was dear, indeed. For the last seven years of his life, Gilles created a private fantasy world, a world that involved children—mostly small fair-haired boys, although small girls were not excluded.

Benedetti lists 36 documented cases of his murders but he admits, as do many others, that there may have been hundreds more. For example, there are only five documented cases of children who were murdered at Gilles' residence in Machecoul, but close to 40 bodies were recovered there in 1437. Gilles developed a gruesome pastime in which he had his aides bring him young children. They would persuade peasants to send their children to the Marshal of France, leading them to believe that they would escape poverty and have a good life. The children, never seen again, could not have been destined for a worse fate.

Gilles developed a ritual torture that hardly ever deviated. He would dress his little victims in fine clothes, get them drunk and then take them to his private rooms. He liked to sodomize them and to ejaculate over their bodies, but he typically hanged them or stabbed them first as he also preferred to have intercourse with them while they were dying. The children were then killed by a variety of methods. Sometimes Gilles himself killed them and sometimes he would watch. Either way, he always enjoyed himself immensely, reportedly laughing raucously throughout. After they were dead, he liked to see them dismembered and decapitated. One witness reported that he would kiss the dead children's heads and discuss with his aides whether today's victim was prettier than yesterday's. If possible, they burned the clothes and bodies in a fireplace, though often the bodies were thrown into a pit.

At the same time that Gilles was murdering children, he maintained an interest in religion and believed himself to be a pious Christian. He developed a plan to create a chapel of his own—the Chapel of the Holy Innocents. To do this, he spent huge sums of money building and furnishing it and providing for priests and a choir. He had himself created Canon of Saint-Hilaire de Poitiers. He cherished his choir boys and they were immune from his sexual and murderous activities.

Gilles was depleting his fortune with abandon. He filled his residences with fine furniture, books and statues and kept a standing army of some 250 men. In 1435, he put on a play in Orléans about his exploits with Joan of Arc, a play that cost him the equivalent of about three million dollars to produce.

Eventually, of course, rumors started to spread that Gilles was kidnapping children and murdering them. Some said that he used their blood for writing, others knew the truth, but there was no redress against the lord of the manor. For a long time, his crimes went largely uninivestigated.

In time, Gilles ran through his fortune. He began to borrow money, to sell off castles and land and to run up huge debts with merchants. In 1435, his relatives grew alarmed at the financial losses of the family. They persuaded the King of France to prohibit the sale of any more assets by Gilles and persuaded the Pope to disavow the Chapel of the Holy Innocents. However, enforcement of these edicts was difficult. The Duke of Brittany was induced to help and attempts were made to seize Gilles' castles. Gilles panicked and rushed to remove evidence of his murders. In October 1437, he had his aides dispose of the bones of at least 40 children at his residence in Machecoul. An interesting footnote to this episode is that one of his aides permitted two noble ladies of the district to watch the clean-up. They did so for enjoyment, not out of moral outrage. Once his relatives had seized Machecoul, they found two skeletons that Gilles' aides had missed, but because their main concern was capturing Gilles' assets, not bringing his perversions to public scrutiny, this did not cause too much trouble.

To enhance his fantasy world, but also to procure new sources of funds, at some point Gilles had begun to dabble in black magic and alchemy. He paid a variety of "experts" for their help and eventually came under the power of François Prelati, an Italian charlatan. None of them helped Gilles in any way, but their efforts later provided ammunition against him at his trial.

The Fall

Gilles' fall was brought about by the Duke of Brittany who, after acquiring much of Gilles' property, now wanted him eliminated. The Duke, together with the Bishop of Nantes, set out to collect evidence to charge, convict and execute the murderous Gilles. Apparently, the Duke did not particularly care that Gilles had orchestrated the death of several hundred children, but the murders were a good way of branding Gilles as a criminal and removing any influence he might have.

Even though Gilles suspected that trouble was brewing, he continued to sexually abuse and murder children. He had frequent depressions, some misgivings and feelings of remorse, but nothing seemed to stop his murderous cravings.

The charges against Gilles were finally drawn up in September 1440 and he was arrested soon afterwards. There were two trials, one by the civil court and the other by the ecclesiastical court. At first he denied the charges, but when threatened with excommunication and torture, he seemed to realize that there was no possibility of acquittal and thereupon made a full, vividly detailed confession of his crimes. He was profusely remorseful, or so he said, and stories have it that he blamed his behavior on the fact that he had such a lenient upbringing. He was convicted of heresy, sodomy and the murder of 140 children. Gilles was sentenced to death on October 25, 1440 and scheduled to be executed the next day. He was excommunicated but only for a short time, for, after making a full confession to his priest, he was readmitted to the Church. He was hanged and a fire lit beneath his feet, but his body was removed before being completely incinerated so that he could be buried in accord with his Christian wishes. He was 36 years old.

Discussion

In explaining the development of Gilles' behavior, Benedetti focuses on the lack of love and affection that Gilles experienced as a child and the disruption that the death of his parents caused. Gilles became an aggressive and brutal individual, but this is what France needed at the time. His personality made him a good soldier.

The end of the war and the death of his grandfather in 1432 caused Gilles to feel rejection once again. His aggression now seemed to turn into self-hate. Benedetti suggests that, rather than committing suicide, when Gilles killed his victims, he was symbolically killing himself over and over again—at least the rejected part of himself. The acceptable part of him was symbolized by his choir boys who he pampered and spoiled. Even the style of the murders symbolizes Gilles' conflicted self—the pattern of attack, fondling and reassurance, sexual assault and finally death shows clearly confused feelings.

The murders failed to resolve Gilles' conflicts. Perhaps they brought him temporary relief, but they also caused him to feel depressed and occasionally remorseful. Perhaps Gilles needed discipline. Benedetti pointed out that under the moral code of conduct imposed by Joan of Arc, Gilles sacrificed his immediate pleasure for a greater purpose. At the end, once Gilles realized that punishment was certain, he submitted to the Church and behaved with dignity.

References

Benedetti, J. *Gilles de Rais.* New York: Stein and Day, 1972.

Masters, R.E.L. and E. Lea. *Perverse Crimes in History.* New York: The Julian Press, 1963.

Chapter 11

The Serial Killers of Nazi Germany

In a certain way, soldiers could be categorized as serial killers, but because their killing is sanctioned by their governments, they are often excused from this category. Not all soldiers make good killers. Based on his combat experience in World War II, Bynum (1982) reckoned that only about 30 percent of soldiers are good at killing. When the critical moment comes, some soldiers will not fire; others pretend that they have and then hide. Most of these types end up being killed or captured. The best killers are often the bravest, most dependable, best liked, most quiet-spoken men. Bynum saw no "loudmouths" in the ranks of good killers, nor any drinkers. A few of the good killers were psychopaths, he said, and these men could not be depended on because they acted on impulse and were therefore unpredictable. Bynum knew one "loner/hunter" type and he made a good sharpshooter.

Soldiers from many nations have committed war crimes that involved serial murder, but few have ever been charged, tried and sentenced for these crimes. Certainly, none have been studied as well as those who committed war crimes on behalf of Germany in the Second World War. There is no typical case of such murders, but in order to illustrate the possible nature of the types of people who committed war crimes that can be considered serial murder, two cases have been chosen for this chapter.

One of the most surprising research findings was that those who committed war crimes were not necessarily psychologically disturbed. From a psychiatric viewpoint, a good proportion of them were relatively normal, but their outward personalities were quite a different story. Based on research by Adorno and co-workers (1950), the type which characterized these individuals was called the *author-*

126

itarian personality. This personality consisted of several traits, including a rigid adherence to conventional middle-class values, an uncritical attitude toward the moral authorities of the group, a tendency to reject and punish people who violate conventional norms, a general hostility toward others, a preoccupation with power and toughness, a tendency to think in rigid categories and the belief that people's fate is mystically determined.

Dicks (1972) found that this type of personality also characterized the Nazi war criminals. Dicks described the type as including (1) a nihilist atheist world view, (2) a bond with an idealized father or father-figure whose values and attitudes had been internalized and which caused conflicts that had not been resolved, (3) a lack of a deep and positive relationship with their mother, (4) an intolerance of tenderness, (5) a cult of manliness, (6) a tendency to antisocial sadism, (7) a tendency to see hostile intent in others when it is not really there and so to feel persecuted and discriminated against and (8) neurotic anxiety.

Dicks interviewed a number of Nazi war criminals in prison and gave examples of many types—the fanatics, the norm setters, the medical humanitarians and the privateers. The following is the case of a man who could be categorized as a fanatic type.

Herr A.

Herr A.'s father was a railway man in Upper Silesia, a region with many German residents, which was claimed by Poland after 1918. Herr A. was born in 1911. His parents were expelled from Silesia in 1920 for refusing to become Polish citizens, but he stayed behind with an aunt. He was a good student in school and became an apprentice to a skilled smith and turner. In 1930, it was clear that the authorities would not allow him to claim his parents' properties, so he emigrated to Breslau (now Wroclaw) where an uncle lived who was a local Nazi leader. Within a year, Herr A. had established himself as a tough street fighter in the Sturmabteilung (SA). In 1933, he was sent to the junior officer school of the Schutzstaffel (SS) where he met his wife and was then posted first to the Esterwege concentration camp and afterward to Camp S where he rose to deputy commandant. Although a model husband and father, at the camp he showed sadistic brutality. He set up whipping blocks for merciless beatings, he trampled victims to death, inserted fire hoses into their mouths and ran water into their bodies until they burst from the pressure and he drowned victims in cesspits. He also tortured inmates by setting their beards and hair on fire and by making the frail ones run across the camp carrying bags of cement.

In 1959, Herr A. was sentenced to lifelong penal servitude by a court in Bonn, Germany. Survivors of the camps and many German anti-Nazis and intellectuals described him as a "most dreaded and bestial character." His nickname in the SS was "Iron George."

When Dicks interviewed him in prison, Herr A. was 56 years old, "with a raw-boned hatchet face and intensely luminous dark eyes, bushy eyebrows and dark, barely graying hair growing low on his temples and forehead—a pretty ugly-looking fellow" (Dicks, p. 97).

Herr A. described the departure of his parents when he was eight years old and how two years later the Polish government forbad them to speak German in schools. All the German children became anti-Polish and the pastor led the German resistance to the Poles. Interestingly, Herr A. insisted that his prison pastor be present at his first interview with Dicks.

As a child during the First World War, Herr A. undoubtedly suffered from the ravages of the economy and society that followed. This insecure period, together with the loss of his parents when he was so young, may have led him to search for father-figures during his life. The local pastor, the smith to whom he was apprenticed and the Nazi uncle in Breslau probably served this role for Herr A. Furthermore, the local SS members in Breslau soon became his reference group rather than his family. Indeed, he made no effort to recontact his parents after they had to leave.

After Hitler became Chancellor of Germany in 1933, Herr A. was chosen as a bodyguard for high-ranking Nazi leaders. In this unit he met and became friendly with Hoess, later the commandant at Auschwitz. In 1934, he accompanied Hitler and SS chief Heinrich Himmler to Bavaria where they liquidated SA leader Ernst Roehm and his associates. Herr A. witnessed this event, though he did not participate in the killing. As Herr A. told Dicks of the executions, he said he was furious at the German judges who refused to rise up and tell Hitler that he could not behave in this way. Herr A. blamed them for allowing people to forget the laws of the land. He told Dicks that he had reported to a magistrate that a man had been sent to his concentration camp in error; the magistrate, Herr A. reported, told him to forget about it.

After his posting to Esterwege, Herr A. was trained by Theodore Eicke, who was known as "Papa." The men were made to watch beatings and executions. SS men who could not or would not obey orders were imprisoned themselves. Herr A., like others, talked of feeling unsuited to the brutality of the work and had conflicts with his conscience, but to tell "Papa" about these feelings risked far too much. One older SS man, a doctor, to whom Herr A. confided his doubts, told him to overcome these feelings and learn to obey.

When he was sent to Camp S, Herr A. felt that he was a member of an elite corps. The camp was run by a succession of notorious torturers, but soon Herr A. identified with this dedicated body of men who controlled vast numbers of cowed people. His superiors punished those who did not act energetically enough and each SS officer tried to set an example to the younger men in their ability to be ruthless. Herr A. remembered one man bringing in a fresh convoy of prisoners who were sentenced to be shot the next day. It became routine and Herr A., like others, eventually became indifferent as he became habituated to the brutality. Yet, he expressed contempt for the SS officers who sat at desks and never soiled their hands.

Herr A. was quite involved with the politics of the time. Jews were irrelevant to him as a group prior to 1938 when Hitler launched his nationwide campaign against them. Herr A. guessed that the war was coming and disliked the nonaggression pact between Hitler and Stalin, but supported Hitler throughout. He also came to realize that he would never be posted to another unit because "I knew too much to be let out.... We knew the intentions of the leadership and we were completely trustworthy to carry them out" (Dicks, p. 103). In fact, he believed in the cause until after his capture by the Americans, at which time he learned that Himmler had run away disguised as a woman and that he had poisoned himself after being apprehended. Himmler, who had told the SS that they were the elect, had shown that he was a coward.

Herr A. told Dicks that he had not disguised himself and gone underground and that he had denied nothing at his trial. Although captured by the Americans, he was turned over to the Soviets to be tried for the war crimes he committed. He was found guilty and sentenced to death. Later in his cell, Herr A. remembered the Ten Commandments and broke down. These were rules he had learned as a child, rules the Germans had forgotten. When the Russians reprieved him, his conversion took hold. In his Siberian labor camp near the Arctic Circle, Herr A. was impressed by the fairness of the Russian guards. They did not strike prisoners and orders for executions were handed down by courts. After Stalin's death in 1953, the camp inmates rebelled, but the camp commandant released him instead of shooting him. Herr A. returned to West Germany where he was arrested and sentenced to another prison term.

Herr A. was boyishly open and easily established rapport with Dicks. He seemed to think that if he was frank, then people would like him. He used the same style with Dicks as he had with the other father-figures in his life, wooing the father-figure with eager devotion and subordination. He had shown increasing obedience to his group and its leaders and he did what they expected even if he privately objected. He had been a good inmate under the Soviets and he had already become the "pet" of the German prison pastor.

This was not what Dicks had expected at all. Herr A. had paranoid, self-pitying, persecuted feelings and an almost childlike lack of guilt and suffering. Dicks could not get Herr A. to talk about his parents and he scarcely mentioned his wife and children. This was important because it seemed that Herr A. had come to blame the Poles for driving his parents away rather than his parents for leaving him. Talking about his parents' desertion might have shattered the operation of this defense mechanism. Dicks sums up Herr A. as "an individual whose need to belong had been perverted, while the resultant anti-parental hate had been displaced to authority-approved targets" (Dicks, p. 108). Herr A. was not a super-aggressive villain, but more like a morally defective child.

Joseph Mengele

Joseph Mengele, a physician, was known as the "Angel of Death" at Auschwitz where he was responsible for the death and mutilation of thousands of prisoners (Posner and Ware, 1986). Most he sent to the gas chambers, a few he personally brutalized and on some he performed what are now generally regarded as senseless medical experiments.

Mengele was born March 16, 1891, in Günzburg, Germany. He was the eldest of the three sons of Karl Mengele, who had built a manufacturing company there. Mengele's father went off to fight in the First World War, and left his wife to run the company. After the war, the company continued to grow.

Mengele's parents quarreled a lot and both were quite cold toward their children. Mengele's nanny was much more influential in his life than his parents were. Mengele was more gifted than his brothers and in high school he was interested in biology and anthropology. Early in life he became determined to succeed, to establish his fame in science so that his name would be in encyclopedias.

When he was six years old, Mengele almost drowned in a barrel of water. He also had a bout of blood poisoning and was stricken with inflammation of the bone marrow. Aside from these, his childhood was not eventful and he suffered no major traumas. After finishing high school in 1930, Mengele decided to study medicine at the University of Munich, with an emphasis on anthropology and genetics. It was there that he was first attracted by the Nazi movement. In 1931 he joined an ex-serviceman's organization, the Stahlhelm, and he joined the Nazi party six years later. Mengele's teachers at medical school advocated the destruction of lives that were considered to be of no social value and this fed into his interest in anthropology and genetics. His doctoral thesis in 1935 was a study of the lower jaw of four racial groups.

Mengele passed his state medical examination in 1936 and took a job at the university medical clinic in Leipzig, where he met the woman who became his first wife. In 1937, he took a position at the Institute for Heredity, Biology and Racial Purity at the University of Frankfurt. The institute's activities reflected the Nazi concern with the selection, engineering, refining and purifying of the German people. Mengele joined the Nazi party in the same year. In May 1938, after a detailed check to determine that there was no Jewish heritage in his family, Mengele was admitted into the SS. Later in 1938, he was awarded a medical degree and he married in July 1939.

Mengele was posted to the war front in the summer of 1940 as a medical officer and he saw combat in June 1941 in the Ukraine. On the Russian front in January 1942, he was awarded an Iron Cross, First Class for his heroism in battle. Mengele returned to Berlin and in May 1943, he was posted to the concentration camp at Auschwitz.

Auschwitz was both an extermination camp and a slave labor camp. Mengele was assigned to inspect those arriving on the trains to decide who would be gassed right away and who could be used for labor. He was described as a ruthless workaholic. There are many stories about Mengele, but a few will illustrate his methods. To eliminate an outbreak of typhus at Auschwitz, Mengele sent all 600 women in one block to the gas chamber. He then had the block disinfected and the women in the next block moved into it and so on throughout the women's camp.

Hoping for scientific fame, Mengele sought out all the twins who arrived at Auschwitz for his research. His studies were particularly barbaric and were of little scientific value. For example, he would perform dissections on twins to examine the similarities in their organs and general development. To do this, the twins had to be killed. He tried exchanging the blood of different pairs of twins and routinely amputated limbs, often without anesthetics.

Many examples of cruelty were later entered in the charges against Mengele, such as torturing, beating and shooting people. Most gruesome was an incident in which he had 300 children burned alive. Mengele seemed to have no qualms about his behavior at the time and when his son visited him in hiding in 1977, he still showed no guilt or remorse. Mengele does not appear to have had any psychiatric disorder, except for one strange behavior—he seems to have been able to co-exist with two contradictory personalities. For example, when a group of Jewish children at Auschwitz developed mouth ulcers, Mengele sought to find a way of curing them. After successfully doing so, he sent the children to the gas chamber. In another documented incident, he carefully assisted a Jewish woman during childbirth, following all of the medical procedures and precautions. Within an hour, however, he sent the mother and her newborn to the gas chamber. Lifton (1985) has called this "doubling," a separation of the good self from the bad self, with each operating independently of the other. Note that this is *not* multiple personality, a neurotic disorder in which the two personalities have amnesia for each other's actions.

Mengele escaped capture and fled to South America after the war. Friends helped him to hide until he reportedly died (allegedly from a stroke while swimming) in Brazil on February 7, 1979. A subsequent exhumation of a body believed to be Mengele's failed to identify him beyond all doubt. In fact, some people believe that he is still alive.

Comment

Charny (1986) has objected to scholars labeling those involved in mass destruction and genocide as "normal." He argued that a guiding criterion for judging whether a person is psychologically healthy or not must be that he holds attitudes that do not denigrate life. If the attitudes held by the Nazis, for example, were espoused by only one person who then tried to kill others in keeping with those attitudes, psychiatrists and psychologists would probably label the person as delusional and psychotic and commit him to a psychiatric hospital. Why then, asked Charny, is an official representative of a *nation* that holds such views, in common with other members of the nation, viewed as normal?

References

Adorno, I.W., E. Frenkel-Brunswik, D.J. Levinson and R.N. Sanford. *The Authoritarian Personality*. New York: Harper and Row, 1950.

Bynum, H.J. Military homicide. In B.L. Danto and A.H. Kutscher (eds.), *The Human Side of Homicide*. New York: Columbia University Press, 1982.

Charny, I.W. Genocide and mass destruction. *Psychiatry* 49:144-157, 1986.

Dicks, H.V. *Licensed Mass Murder*. New York: Basic Books, 1972.

Lifton, R.J. What made this man Mengele? *New York Times Magazine*, July 21, 1985, p. 22.

Posner, G.L. and J. Ware. *Mengele*. New York: McGraw-Hill, 1986.

Chapter 12

Mafia Killers

Members of the Mafia often murder and many meet the criteria for serial murder. In this chapter we will illustrate Mafia serial murderers with a low-level "hit man" and a mob boss.

Joey: A Hit Man

Joey, a hit man for the Mafia, admits to killing 38 people, all of whom were members of the mob (Joey, 1973). Thirty-five were contracted murders and three were for personal revenge. He helped the mob in a variety of other ways too, smuggling narcotics and tobacco, hijacking trucks, bootlegging perfumes, records, running card games and numbers, fencing stolen goods, booking bets and making pornographic movies. But his specialty was killing. He reckoned that he had earned roughly $4,000,000 for this service over the years. By the time he wrote his autobiography, the mob was using him less frequently because his excessive gambling made him unreliable.

Joey was questioned by the police in 17 murder cases (he claimed guilt for only three), brought before a grand jury seven times, and held for trial three times. He was never once convicted.

Joey's Early Life

Joey was born in 1932 in the Bronx, the second son of second-generation Eastern European immigrants. His father was a reasonably successful bootlegger and his mother was a typical housewife. After the end of Prohibition, Joey's father became a numbers banker.

Joey's world changed when his father was sent to prison for six years for murdering two men who were sent to take over his operation. Joey's mother had never worked outside the home and this being the Depression, was unable to find a job. They lived for a while on what Joey's older brother could steal. Joey was then sent to a state orphanage. He spent eight months there and then more than four years in foster homes. He was sent back home when he was 10.

Joey remembers good and bad foster home experiences. A good one was on the Upper East Side of Manhattan where he said he was made to feel like a real son. However, the state took him away from this home after a year.* He also remembers the bad ones, such as one in Manhattan's Hell's Kitchen where he got into fights with his foster parents' son and was beaten continually by the father of the family.

Back home at the age of 10, life had changed. His mother was dying from cancer and she wasted away from 170 to 70 pounds at the time of her death. His father, who was hardly ever at home and probably still involved in criminal activities, died a year later. Joey says, "I didn't miss him when he was dead; I missed him while he was alive" (p. 29). Joey lived with his older brother for a year and then, when his brother got married, he moved into his own apartment when he was 16.

Joey first worked with the mob when he was 11. A local boss set him up with a table on the street to run numbers. (The police, presumably paid off, never interfered.) He stole rationing stamps and siphoned off gas from cars and was making nearly $100 a day at the age of 11. He had his first lover at age 14 and by the following year was controlling the numbers racket in his area, with 40 runners, a nice car and an income of $500 a day.

After two years of controlling the numbers in his area, three men tried to take over Joey's business. He hit one of them and told them to clear off. Two weeks later, noticing he was being followed, Joey went into a store to buy a baseball bat and then walked up to the men and started swinging. He was inflicting great damage when a cop arrived on the scene. The judge gave Joey the option of four years in a detention center or joining the army. Joey chose to enlist.

Joey liked the army. He was taught how to use guns and how to plan. He was sent to Korea where he fought well. On one occasion, Joey and his two best friends were on a mission and one was killed. Joey and the other friend carried the body 70 miles back to base so that it could be buried properly. On another occasion, Joey and his friend saw an American colonel captured by North Koreans and they killed his captors and spent six days getting the colonel back to safety. Later the colonel offered him lifetime security in the army, but Joey declined. Joey says that he was never really scared in combat, but that he was wary and he has maintained that trait all his life.

---

*Joey kept in touch with this family, sending them gifts and helping out with the father when he had a stroke.

Joey killed his first man when he was 16. He admits that he had always been violent and that he fought a lot, but he had never thought of killing anyone. One day, a mobster offered Joey a contract. Joey thought about it for the rest of the day, decided he "was going to be a man" and after a couple of days of planning, walked up to the victim in the street, shot him in the head and walked away. He had made $5000 that easily, while his older brother was working 10 hours a day in a warehouse for $24 a week!

After his tour in the service, Joey moved to California where he began working with mobsters. Soon he was making hits. The most Joey was ever offered for a hit was $50,000 and he is quite specific about the rules. The full amount of the money must be paid in advance. After the contract is made, the contractor can rescind it, but cannot get his money back. The hit man must guarantee not to talk, even if caught, and the contractor must pay all legal fees and take care of the hit man's family if he is sent to prison. A victim is not to be killed in his own home, in a church, or in front of his family; you do not torture or rob the victim; and you do not harm his family.

By 1958, Joey was married and his wife was pregnant. Joey had smuggled narcotics into the United States from Mexico and his contacts decided to kill Joey rather than pay him. Joey was out when they called, so they beat up Joey's pregnant wife and left her hemorrhaging. She was dead by the time the neighbors got her to the hospital. Joey was in Reno, Nevada, but they found him there and they beat him up badly, leaving him paralyzed from the neck down. When Joey found out that his wife had been murdered, he vowed to recover. He also says, "That was the day I stopped caring whether I lived or died. That was the day I lost all fear of death" (p. 96). Surgery restored his health and Joey stalked the killers. He found the men and killed them painfully, using flat-nosed bullets (after being fired, flat-nosed bullets become twice the diameter of their original size, creating a large entry site and massive internal destruction). At the time he was writing his autobiography, Joey was waiting for the boss who ordered the attack to get out of prison so that he could kill him too.

Joey has remarried and he takes care to tell us that he would never abuse his wife. He does not want to live with someone who is afraid of him or who will turn him in to the police. Joey gives her about 40 percent of what he earns and she invests it.

Why does Joey kill? He says that the money is good, that being a hit man brings him status, that killing proves his loyalty and courage and, finally, because he enjoys it. He likes the awesome power he has as a hit man, deciding whether someone lives or dies.

Discussion

Joey's early life is full of clues to his development as a serial killer. First, his father was a criminal, probably a low-status member of the mob. The friends of the family and the kids Joey associated with were also probably involved with the mob. Indeed, a friend of the family offered Joey his first job in numbers. Thus, Joey's criminal career is an example of the *subcultural criminal*, a person born into a criminal subculture, who is socialized into that culture.

Second, Joey's early life was traumatic—his father being imprisoned when he was five; being sent to an orphanage and living in foster homes until age 10; being beaten in some of the foster homes; his mother dying when he was 14 and his father a year later. These are the kinds of traumas that we find in the childhoods of violent people.

However, Joey's traumas, though severe, are not quite the same as the brutality that was experienced by some of the more vicious serial killers whose lives are described in this book. And, correspondingly, Joey is not as vicious as they are. He has killed only mobsters and he kills according to rules. You may think at first that killing by rules does not make the killing any more excusable. However, remember that Joey was a soldier and fought in Korea. Soldiers kill by rules. There are killings that are allowed and killings that are not. For example, torture of the enemy is not allowed (even though this does not mean that it doesn't happen). Killing prisoners and civilians is not allowed. Killing in the wrong way can result in a court martial for "crimes against humanity" or a similar charge. Joey was a good soldier and he might have made a great soldier had he not been socialized into the mob before serving in the military.

The cover of Joey's autobiography says "Joey is a son-of-a-bitch, alive and a functioning member of our sick society." Of course, a publisher wants to sell books and so engages in embellishment and sensationalism. On the other hand, given the family into which he was born, Joey seems pretty much like an ordinary person to me, the kind who was a good soldier and who might have had a fine military career. If Joey had been born to a career soldier, he might be a recognized military leader by now. But Joey lived in a mob family, so he became a hit man. Lawyers have children who become lawyers; plumbers have children who become plumbers. Childhood socialization is a powerful experience.

Sam Giancana: A Mob Boss

Sam Giancana grew up in Chicago, joined a teenage gang and graduated to become a hit man for the renowned Al Capone. By the time he was 20, he had killed dozens of men and had participated in the St. Valentine's Day Massacre. He soon rose to dominate Mafia activities west of the Mississippi, until his assassination in 1975. A police report described him as a "snarling, sarcastic, ill-tempered, sadistic psychopath" (Sifakis, 1987, p. 138).

What is of interest here is not a detailed listing of his criminal activities but what we can find out about his early years that may explain, to some extent, his adult criminal and murderous behavior.

Early Years

In the biography of Sam Giancana co-authored by his brother and godson, we learn that he was born on May 24, 1908, to Antonio and Antonia Giancana in Chicago's Little Italy (Giancana and Giancana, 1992) and was christened Salvatore Giancana. Sam had an elder sister, Lena. His parents were natives of the Sicilian village of Castelvetrano.

By 1910, the Italian population of Chicago had grown to over 40,000 people. Sam's father, like many of the new immigrants, turned to peddling food from a cart in the city. Sam's mother died after a miscarriage on March 14, 1910. Sam was not yet two. Sam is described by his biographers as stubborn, independent and inquisitive and, after his mother's death, as sullen and quiet.

Sam's father was quickly remarried (to Mary Leonardi). He appears to have beaten his new wife regularly. Mary had children in 1912 and 1914. Sam's father was a harsh disciplinarian and apparently he saw his son as rebellious and meddlesome. His solution was to beat him. Sam's biographers describe an incident when Sam was six in which his father chained him to an oak tree behind the tenement and beat him with a razor strap until Sam bled and then left him tied there for the evening. The father made him sleep on the floor in the kitchen thereafter and beat him regularly over the next four years.

At the age of 10, when he was in fifth grade, Sam's teachers decided that he was a hopeless delinquent and he was sent to a reformatory for six months. After Sam was released, he lived on the streets, sleeping in abandoned cars or under porches and stealing food. He soon fell in with a gang that became known as the "42s." They graduated from petty theft, to auto theft, to robbery and murder. The neighborhood viewed them with both alarm and with pride. The authorities in the city were mainly Irish-Americans and the Italian-Americans had little trust in and respect for the authorities. The gangs reminded the Italian immigrants of the type of law and order they were used to in the old country and they liked the fact that the gangs stood up to the authorities.

Sam soon rose in the gang's hierarchy and was respected as one of the best getaway car drivers. By the time he was 13, Sam was known as the wildest and most daring of the 42s and was given the nickname "Mooney," which he himself changed to "Momo."

Soon Sam was recruited by the crime bosses and at the age of 15 he was running sugar and alcohol for Diamond Joe Esposito. When Al Capone took over the territory, he recruited the 17-year-old Sam to help eliminate his rivals.

Sam's first prison term was 30 days for auto theft in 1925 and after his release he went to confront his father. At first, his father tried to act as the bully he once was, but Sam held a kitchen knife to his father's throat and told him never to touch him again or he would kill him. After that, Sam's father became submissive to his son. In fact, he allowed him to be the head of the family.

Maturity

Sam came under the wing of Tony Accardo and Paul Ricca, moving up through the ranks of the Chicago outfit under their tutelage. By the 1950s, as the leadership grew old, Accardo and Ricca promoted Sam to operating head of the mob. Sam, of course, promoted his old buddies from the 42 gang and they became known as the Youngbloods.

As they expanded their operations and took over more of the rackets, Sam's prestige grew. He produced huge sums of money for the mob and so earned its respect—that is, as long as the money continued to flow in. Sam became friends with entertainment figures such as Frank Sinatra and Sifakis (1987) claims that he shared a mistress for a time with President John Kennedy.

Sam's interests extended to Las Vegas, Mexico and Cuba and he may have become involved with the CIA plot to overthrow Fidel Castro in Cuba. It was this last involvement that doomed him. Paul Ricca was already disturbed by Sam's murders, his love affairs and his problems with the FBI. As such, Ricca demoted Sam and left him with only gambling enterprises in Mexico. In 1975, as the details of his possible involvement with the CIA were becoming known, Sam was ordered to testify before a Senate investigating committee. On June 19, 1975, Sam was in the basement kitchen of his Oak Park, Illinois home, cooking a snack before bedtime, when an unknown visitor shot him once in the back of the head and six more times in the front. After Sam's assassination, CIA Director William Colby denied any CIA involvement.

Comments

There are two interesting features of Sam Giancana's childhood. First the death of his mother when he was two and the physical abuse by his father may have provided the source of his violent rage. Interestingly, however, he did not murder his father; rather he simply threatened him and cowed him into a submissive role for the rest of his life. It seems evident that abusive childhoods can lead to abusive adults. Indeed, Sam was almost as brutal a disciplinarian to his younger brother and his own children as his father had been to him and he committed rape at will—alone and in gangs.

Secondly, because he belonged to a strong subculture in Chicago's Little Italy, Sam easily joined a gang with ties to organized crime and, being good at what he did, he became one of the leaders in the group. Quay (1965) proposed a typology of delinquents which included the *unsocialized psychopathic* type, with aggressive and uncontrollable impulses and a general disregard for others; the *disturbed neurotic* type, with feelings of depression and inferiority; and the *socialized subcultural* type, with a tendency to follow the norms of their peers who happen to be delinquent. Sam clearly fits into the socialized subcultural type. Though he understandably rebelled against his brutal father, he adhered to the values and customs of his peer group. Thus, his rage could be channeled into organized crime, with its own code of honor and brutality, a microcosm that is a good example of what Wolfgang and Ferracuti (1969) called *subcultures of violence.*

References

Giancana, S. and C. Giancana. *Double Cross.* New York: Warner Books, 1992.
Joey. *Killer: Autobiography of a Hit Man for the Mafia.* Chicago: Playboy Press, 1973.
Quay, H. *Juvenile Delinquency.* Princeton, NJ: Van Nostrand, 1965.
Sifakis, C. *The Mafia Encyclopedia.* New York: Facts on File, 1987.
Wolfgang, M. and F. Ferracuti. *The Subculture of Violence.* New York: Tavistock, 1969.

Chapter 13

Terrorists

It is hard to define what a terrorist is, for today's "terrorist" may become tomorrow's elected president or prime minister. Terrorism generates a high level of fear in society, has a coercive purpose and requires a human audience (Cooper, 1982). Terroristic acts are committed to impress others and they may also have a symbolic meaning.

Sometimes terrorism involves assassination and Cooper (1982) noted that people are assassinated because of what they represent. The victim is killed in order to influence events. All assassinations are not necessarily terroristic acts. For example, of the eight assassinations or attempted assassinations of U.S. presidents or presidents-elect between 1835 and 1963, only one counts as an act of terrorism—the attempt on President Truman's life in 1950 by Oscar Callazo and Griselio Torresola, who acted on behalf of the militantly pro-independence Puerto Rican Nationalist Party. Torresola was killed during the attempt, but at his trial, Callazo said that he had hoped that Truman's death might result in a revolution in Puerto Rico.

Compared to kidnapping, assassination is an economical undertaking for terrorists. It requires few personnel and little in the way of support services. There is no need for safe hideouts, elaborate communication systems, negotiations and escape. Cooper (1982) noted that the assassins employed by political movements tend to be criminal and psychopathic, but rarely psychotic. They may be seen as "true believers" and misfits in the larger society.

One of the most successful modern terrorist groups was the Baader-Meinhof Gang in Germany and the life history of its co-founder, Ulrike Meinhof, illustrates the career of a terrorist.

Ulrike Meinhof

Ulrike Meinhof was one of the leading terrorists in West Germany in the 1970s. She took part in numerous bank robberies, assassinations and bomb attacks. Meinhof was eventually captured, but she committed suicide in prison before sentencing (Demaris, 1977).

Early Years

Meinhof was born on October 7, 1934 in Oldenburg, West Germany. She grew up in the midst the of violence of the Second World War. Her father, a museum director, died of cancer when she was six years old. Her mother was an art teacher and she sent her daughter to a Roman Catholic parochial school. After her mother's death, Meinhof was reared by a foster parent, Professor Renate Riemeck, who encouraged her academic studies and guided her toward a liberal political viewpoint.

Meinhof was a good student and went to the University of Munich. While there, she got involved with the ban-the-bomb movement, one of the leaders of which was her foster-father. She also met Klaus Roehl who was the publisher of the Hamburg magazine *Konkret*, which had become the voice of the radical German student movement. She started to write for the magazine, became its editor-in-chief and married Roehl. A year later she gave birth to twins. In the 1960s, she achieved celebrity status as a provocative radical, writer and television polemicist. Meinhof and Roehl had traveled to East Germany and secured funds to support the magazine, but the Communist Party there gave them free rein over its contents. Demaris (1977) describes the magazine as more like *Playboy* than *Pravda*. In 1965, Meinhof developed a brain tumor and a clamp had to be inserted into her brain to ease the pressure.

Conversion

Meinhof became tired of words of protest, but she was still opposed to violence. Her young brother-in-law once pulled out a revolver in the woods and shot it, causing Meinhof to have a hysterical fit and a mild nervous breakdown. As a result, she would not talk to her brother-in-law for a year. Her disgust with her way of life grew and she divorced Roehl and moved with her daughters from Hamburg to West Berlin.

There she joined the Ausser Parlamentarische Opposition (or APO), led by Rudi Dutschke. The APO was anti-American, anti-imperialist and anti-establishment. After members of the group were arrested for firebombing two warehouses in April 1968 as a protest against the Vietnam War, Meinhof visited them in prison and was especially impressed with Andreas Baader. Born in May 1943, Baader was the happy-go-lucky type who had a criminal history. He moved the group from theory into action. He then became allied with Meinhof and gradually assumed the leadership of the group that came to be known as the Baader-Meinhof Gang.

Of the original 22 members, nearly half were women, as were eight of the next 20 recruits. Baader was sentenced to three years for the firebombings but was released after serving nine months, pending final sentencing. He failed to return to the courts and began an underground existence. Meinhoff continued to write and lecture and her first violent act was to take some members of the gang and vandalize her ex-husband's house. They destroyed the furnishings, defaced the walls and urinated on the bed.

Baader was captured in April 1970, but Meinhof and other gang members attacked the guards who were transporting him, using tear-gas and gunfire to free him. Two guards and a librarian were injured. Two weeks later, Meinhof, Baader and a few other members went to Jordan to train at an al-Fatah Palestinian training camp. Returning to Germany, the gang's wave of terror began in earnest: 80 bombings and arson assaults in West Berlin alone in 1970, including three simultaneous bank robberies on September 29, 1970. A week later, all three banks were bombed. In 1971, the radical left, including the Baader-Meinhof Gang, was responsible for 555 acts of terrorism throughout Europe. In one week in May 1972, 15 bombs exploded in West Germany, damaging the headquarters of the U.S. Fifth Army, the Augsburg Police Headquarters and the Munich Criminal Investigation Office. Demaris calls the gang the most successful terrorists in Europe after the Irish Republican Army in Northern Ireland.

Capture and Death

Baader was captured on June 1, 1972 and Meinhof on June 15, after a friend gave her away to the authorities. Meinhof was kept in solitary confinement, with the lights permanently on, despite protests by her lawyers that this was cruel and inhumane treatment. She led three hunger strikes: for a month beginning in January 1973, for seven weeks beginning in May and for five months beginning in September 1974, during which one of the prisoners died despite forced feeding.

The major trial of the Baader-Meinhof Gang began in June 1975, despite protests over the fact that the defense attorneys had been barred from the court and the new attorneys had no time to prepare. When the trial began, the prisoners refused to participate and were tried in absentia.

The imprisonment and hunger strikes had weakened all the defendants. Meinhof was forgetful, had trouble articulating, concentrating and even understanding clearly. She felt weak and had headaches and had lost 28 pounds. Finally, on May 8, 1976, while the other members of the gang were exercising, she hanged herself from the bars of her cell with a white prison towel. The guards found her on Sunday.

Comment

The critical events from Meinhof's early life are the death of her father when she was six and the death of her mother soon after. She also lived through the Second World War, with the persecution of millions of Germans by the Nazis in the years leading up to the war and the destruction wrought by the Allied attacks. Meinhof's childhood was largely lived during wartime. Her life settled down until, at the age of 31 she was discovered to have a brain tumor. Once she had become a left-wing radical, her peer group shaped her behavior. Perhaps her early life experiences and possible brain damage made her susceptible to the influences of the radicals with whom she began to associate.

References

Cooper, H.H.A. Terroristic fads and fashions. In B.L. Danto and A.H. Kutscher (eds.), *The Human Side of Homicide.* New York: Columbia University Press, 1982.
Demaris, O. *Brothers in Blood.* New York: Scribners, 1977.

Chapter 14

Outlaws and Pirates

One type of serial killer almost always excluded by writers on the topic is the armed robber. Some scholars ignore serial killing motivated by financial profit. However, such serial killers may be even more common than the well-publicized sexually motivated killers. In this chapter we will present cases of outlaws and pirates, two types of serial killers common in times past.

John Murrell

American history has witnessed incredible periods of lawlessness. Wellman (1961) has described the lives of some of the better-known outlaws, starting with William Clarke Quantrill in Civil War times and ending with the death of Pretty Boy Floyd at the hands of the FBI in 1934.

However, of all the lawless figures of America's early days, Wellman focused on John Murrell as perhaps the most notorious murderer. Some details of Murrell's life remain unknown and it is occasionally difficult to separate truth from legend. Nevertheless, he was probably born in 1804 in a tavern owned by his parents near Columbia, Tennessee, about 40 miles south of Nashville (Wellman, 1964; Phares, 1941). His father, an itinerant preacher, was henpecked by his wife and therefore was hardly ever at home. His mother ran the tavern and appears to have had numerous affairs, and perhaps even worked as a prostitute. In fact, her promiscuity was such that there are doubts as to the identity of Murrell's biological father. She trained all of her children to steal, especially from the suitcases and trunks of the men she entertained in bed.

Once, when Murrell was 16, his mother was entertaining one Daniel Crenshaw, who incidentally is suspected of being Murrell's real father. Murrell decided to steal money from both Crenshaw and

his mother and to take off for Nashville. A few days later, he ran into
Crenshaw there. Rather than being angry with the young man,
Crenshaw decided to take him on as a partner. They stole four horses
and set off for Georgia. On the way they met a young man whom
they killed for his horse and over a thousand dollars.

Crenshaw trained Murrell in the art of crime and introduced him
to the different pleasures the proceeds could buy. As Murrell matured, he moved from being the student to being the leader. In 1821,
the two passed through a small town in Alabama. With the exception
of some white guards, the town seemed abandoned. It turned out
that because of a rumor, the black slaves were planning a revolt, and
so all the white people had closed their businesses and locked
themselves into their houses. This planted the idea in Murrell's
mind that such a situation would be ideal for a large-scale crime.
What if he could incite thousands of slaves to revolt and, during the
turmoil, ransack whole towns—the homes, banks and warehouses?
How could this be done?

While slowly making plans and arranging all the details, Murrell
continued his criminal career. He stole horses and killed their riders
and he disseminated counterfeit money. Murrell met an itinerant
preacher, Elijah Carter, from whom he learned how to lead revivalist
meetings. Later he would run such meetings while his men stole the
belongings of the people in attendance.

Murrell's most despicable criminal activity was stealing slaves and
selling them, only to steal them back again (often with the slaves'
cooperation). He used their knowledge of the "Underground Rail-
road" to freedom in the North to persuade slaves to leave of their
own free will, after which he would urge them to let him sell them
a few times before getting them to freedom. Hardly any of the slaves
survived, for after a few cycles, Murrell would kill them, gut their
bodies, fill them with sand and sink them in the local rivers. He is
thought to have killed more than a hundred slaves in this way.

Murrell was arrested for the first time for horse theft in 1831. He
was branded on his left thumb with the letters "HT" for horse thief,
given 39 lashes on his bare back, placed in a pillory for two hours
on three successive days and imprisoned for a year. Thereafter, he
always wore gloves to hide the brand on his thumb. Murrell used his
time in prison to plan the slave uprising; he realized that he would
need a central planning group (the "Grand Council"), a network of
aides (the "Strykers") and the cooperation of a secret slave army. He
called his secret organization the "Mystic Clan." After being a model
prisoner and obtaining his release, Murrell set about accumulating

wealth and recruiting men for his secret network. Yet he also created an aura of respectability to divert suspicion from himself, building a grand house in Denmark, Tennessee. He also installed a lover who he presented as "Mrs. Murrell" and dressed in the most fashionable clothes of superior cut and material.

The plan might have succeeded except for Virgil Stewart. In January 1834, this young man was visiting a friend, the Reverend John Henning, who had just had some slaves stolen. Stewart offered to track them down. Soon after leaving, he ran into Murrell. As they rode, Murrell took a liking to Stewart and, rather than killing him for his horse and money, decided to recruit him into the organization. It took Stewart several days to realize who his riding partner was, but then he decided to pretend that he was indeed a criminal and that he was willing to join the organization. Stewart learned that the Grand Council had some 40 members and Murrell dictated at one point a list of over 450 men who were the Strykers. After Stewart managed to leave Murrell, he reported back to the Reverend Henning. Henning then rounded up a posse and captured Murrell on February 7, 1834, taking him to the county seat of Madison County, Tennessee.

Murrell escaped before his trial but was soon recaptured in Florence, Alabama. He was tried in July 1834, for slave stealing, with Stewart as the chief witness. Murrell's lawyers (he could afford the best) tried to portray Stewart as a criminal member of the gang, but the jury found Murrell guilty. He was sentenced to 10 years hard labor in the Tennessee State Penitentiary. Wellman (1964) notes that there are no details as to what happened to Murrell during those 10 years, but prison life was very hard and Murrell came out a broken man.

Some legends have Murrell moving to Mississippi with some of his old gang and taking up his life of crime again. Wellman argues that he came out in bad health and was practically an imbecile. He had learned to be a blacksmith while in prison. He settled in Pikesville in Bledsoe County, Tennessee, where he worked as a blacksmith until his early death, probably from tuberculosis. Wellman received a letter from a resident of the town who, as a little girl, knew that Murrell was buried in the cemetery at Smyrna and she remembered that Murrell's smithy was still in use.

What happened to the slave rebellion and massive theft without Murrell's leadership? Although Murrell's supporters tried to present Stewart as a criminal and some writers on the period still do so, Stewart published a book in early 1835 entitled *A History of the*

Detection, Conviction and Designs of John A. Murrell, the Great Western Land Pirate, telling of the planned uprising on Christmas Day, 1835. Slave owners, alerted to the plan, watched their slaves carefully and several heard their slaves talking of the revolt. By June, slaves were being arrested and questioned and soon some of the white ringleaders were rounded up. Lynch law went into full effect and, after cursory trials, many were executed. The majority of the organization fled to other parts of the country.

Phoolan Devi

Of course, outlaws are not just a Western phenomenon and one achieved notoriety recently in India. In a study of one region of India for a two-year period in the 1980s, Sharma (1985) identified 228 women convicted of murder. (We are not told how many men were convicted of murder during this period.) Three of these committed mass murder and three serial murder. All three serial murderers were criminal outlaws, or in Indian terms, members of dacoit gangs.

One of the three, a 26-year-old gang leader named Phoolan Devi, was described by the media as the "dacoit of the decade." Sharma described her as of small stature, with dirty unplaited hair kept in place with a cloth tied around her head and as moody, brash and irritable. She was born in a rural area to a poor family of a persecuted Hindu caste. She was married off at the age of 13 to a man 20 years her elder and the rejection by her family and husband led her to collude with a dacoit gang leader to rob her cousins. She was arrested for this, jumped bail and became the lover of the gang leader. After her lover was killed by police, Devi's gang massacred 20 villagers whom she held responsible for her lover's capture. She then became the lover of another gang leader and soon became established as the leader herself. She then led the gang on a two-year spree of crimes until her arrest in February 1983. So great was Phoolan Devi's popularity with the poor of India that all charges against her were dropped in a political deal. A recent film biography, *The Bandit Queen*, has received rave reviews.

Ned Low

There have been many infamous pirates, both American and from other nations. One of the most infamous was Edward (Ned) Low (Snow, 1944). Low went to sea at an early age and, while visiting Boston during his travels, he liked it so much that he settled there, working in a shipyard. He married in 1714, but his first child died and then during childbirth, his wife also died, leaving him with one daughter. His behavior changed after these losses and he was fired from the shipyard. He signed on a ship as a member of the crew, but under the harsh treatment of the captain, some of the crew rebelled and decided to become pirates with Low as captain.

In early 1722, Low first joined up with another pirate, George Lowther, and plundered ships in the Caribbean, until Lowther got tired of Low's cruelty and gave him his own ship and crew. Low then sailed up to the North Atlantic and down to South America to continue his plundering.

Snow gives several examples of Low's cruelty. For example, after capturing a Portuguese ship near Surinam, he had the Portuguese sailors tortured to force them to tell where the crew had hidden their treasure. (The captain of the ship had actually thrown it into the sea.) Low tied the captain to the mast, sliced off his lips, broiled them and made the Portuguese crew eat them. Then Low and his own men murdered every officer and sailor on the Portuguese ship. Low often had his men butcher entire crews. In another incident, Low captured a ship off Block Island in the North Atlantic and cut and slashed the captain, finally decapitating him. Later that day, Low killed the captain of another ship, roasted his heart and made the captain's mate eat it.

Low managed to escape capture for a while, but in May 1724, a French warship found him and three others adrift in a small boat. It appears that Low had murdered his quartermaster and his crew had risen against him and set him afloat. The French took him to Martinique where they tried and executed him.

Anne Bonny

One of the most interesting pirates is Anne Bonny, a woman who brought brains and style to pirating. Anne's father, William Cormac, was a respected lawyer in Cork, Ireland, who had an affair with his serving maid, Peg Brennan, and made her pregnant. Rather than throwing her out, he set Peg up in her own house. His wife was also pregnant and her family, the Sweeneys, were outraged. On March 8, 1700, the Sweeneys ran the Cormacs out of Cork. That was the day when Peg gave birth to Anne. Cormac fled to London, sent for Peg and Anne and emigrated to America, settling in Charleston, South Carolina.

Cormac started a trading firm and bought a large plantation. By the time Anne was 10, he was one of the richest men in the area. Up until this time, Anne was a well-behaved child, with tutors, fine clothes, horses to ride and her own slaves. But at age 10, she began to change. She insisted on attending the public school where she became the leader of the school yard by battling the boys and girls. She became friendly with an American Indian hunter on the plantation and learned how to throw knives and to shoot. When she was 13 she began to explore the docks of Charleston and joined the youthful gangs.

At home, there was a servant who detested Anne and who one day spilled hot food over her. When Anne jumped up and slapped her, the servant grabbed a knife. Anne whipped out the knife that she habitually carried and killed her. Since it was self-defense, Anne was let off without even a scolding. But the incident sobered the 14-year-old Anne for a few months. She abandoned her tomboy ways and behaved in a more lady-like manner.

Anne took the first of her lovers when she was 15. One of them, the son of a wealthy planter, told Anne's father of his conquest and tried to force a marriage, to which the father was agreeable. Anne beat the young man severely with a chair and none of her lovers ever talked about their affairs with Anne to her father again. Anne began visiting the docks again, but this time she was dressed as a lady and was accompanied by the leading pirate captains.* She met a young smuggler, James Bonny, and was so attracted to him that she agreed to marry him. They hoped that her father would give them money as a wedding gift so they could buy a ship which they would then use for smuggling. On hearing the news of the wedding, Anne's mother died and her father threw her out, even shooting at her when she tried to visit him. Anne fought back, setting fire to the house, whereupon her father swore out a warrant for her arrest. Two pirate friends saved her by helping her to escape to New Providence (now Nassau in the Bahamas), which at that time was a pirate haven.

Anne, now 16, arrived in New Providence and quickly established her reputation. As she walked from the ship into town, a drunk reached for a gun, but she shot his ear off before he could fire. James Bonny set to work fishing for turtles. Anne, however, looked around for a wealthy lover. She settled on Chidley Bayard, a trader dealing in pirate booty, who already had a lover, Maria Vargas. On the day they arrived back in New Providence from a trip to Jamaica, Anne

---

* Piracy was not always considered a dishonorable profession and some pirates (or freebooters) attained eminence in the local society.

and Maria got into a fight that developed into a duel with swords, ending when Anne killed Maria. Anne took Maria's place as Bayard's lover.

Soon, however, she was attracted to John Rackam, better known as Calico Jack. When a new governor, Woodes Rogers, arrived in New Providence from England, intent on bringing some law and order to the island, Anne, Jack and Captain Charles Vane decided to escape by ship and remain pirates. Within days, Anne was sexually assaulted by a sailor on board and she promptly killed him in a duel. Thereafter she was treated with great respect. Soon Captain Vane was voted out of command and Calico Jack installed in his place, even though the crew knew that Anne was really the one in charge.

Anne became pregnant and left the ship for a while, but gave birth prematurely to an infant who died shortly thereafter. Jack arranged to take Anne back to New Providence, where it had been arranged that they would not be prosecuted for the theft of some gold that they had taken from Bayard. However, James Bonny brought charges that Calico Jack had stolen his wife and the Governor forbad Jack and Anne to continue as lovers. Rather than submit, they sailed away, but not before looking for Bonny in order to kill him and wounding his housemate.

From July 1719 on, Jack and Anne successfully plundered ships in the Caribbean. With Anne directing, the crew relied on terror more than fighting to subdue their prey. However, Jack drifted slowly into alcoholism and became addicted to smoking half-green tobacco, and eventually became impotent. Anne assumed control of the crew, taking all of them as lovers, with the exception of one whom she discovered was a woman in male disguise named Mary Read. Anne's promiscuity at first could be seen simply as the result of a strong sexual drive. But now her contempt for men was evident as she used sex to dominate them. Indeed, her closest confidants were a homosexual sailor and Mary Read.

In early 1720, Anne's vessel and several other pirate ships returned to New Providence to help the Governor successfully fight off the Spanish invasion. They then returned to piracy. Many stories have been told about Anne, not all them true. In a vote to depose Calico Jack as captain, Anne is supposed to have shot one pirate dead who proposed to vote against him. She is also said to have shot an informer dead as he was having intercourse with her. There are stories of her freeing the slaves from a captured slave ship in Cuba and releasing a shipload of lunatics in Jamaica. On capturing a prison ship, she released the prisoners and fell in love with the ship's doctor, Michael Radcliffe, who had been locked up for opposing the captain's brutality.

Anne's life of piracy, however, quickly came to an end. Her ship was destroyed in a storm with Radcliffe lost at sea and Anne, Jack and the few remaining crew members were reduced to stealing food to stay alive. They were captured by the Governor of Jamaica and tried in November 1720. The men were hanged, but Anne was pregnant (with Radcliffe's child) and Radcliffe arrived having survived the shipwreck after all. With public sentiment turning in her favor and a letter from the Governor of New Providence attesting how she had helped defeat the Spanish, Anne was pardoned on condition that she give up piracy and leave the West Indies. Anne and Radcliffe sailed for Norfolk, Virginia, after which there is no trace of them.

Comment

Outlaws and pirates were common in times past and it was not necessarily deviant individuals who joined their ranks. Typically, those who were poor and had few legitimate avenues for success in the world chose a life of crime as a way to escape poverty. Ned Low's decision to become a pirate seems to have been made during a time of despair after the loss of his wife and child. Anne Bonny, on the other hand, seems to have been drawn into pirating by the excitement of the life. The wonder is that she took so easily to that life, acting firmly and decisively at the tender age of 16.

References

Carlova, J. *Mistress of the Seas*. London: Jarrolds, 1965.
Phares, R. *Reverend Devil*. New Orleans: Pelican Publishing Company, 1941.
Sharma, S. Mass murder by women. *Indian Journal of Criminology* 13(1):11-15, 1985.
Snow, E.R. *Pirates and Buccaneers of the Atlantic Coast*. Boston: Yankee, 1944.
Wellman, P.I. *A Dynasty of Western Outlaws*. Garden City, NY: Doubleday, 1961.
Wellman, P.I. *Spawn of Evil*. Garden City, NY: Doubleday, 1964.

Chapter 15

Murder in the 'Hood

Some youths join gangs and many of the members of juvenile gangs eventually turn to murder. Kody Scott, a member of the Crips in Los Angeles, recently wrote his autobiography (Scott, 1993) and I have summarized his life in this chapter.

Kody Scott was born in Los Angeles, in 1964 or thereabouts, the second youngest of a family of six (three brothers and two sisters). As a teenager he found out that his father was not Mr. Scott. Kody's mother had had an affair with Dick Bass, a football player for the Los Angeles Rams, during a period when she and her husband were not getting along well. Scott wanted her to have an abortion, but she refused. The result was that he hated the child that was born— Kody.[*] Kody remembered that Mr. Scott never took him along when he went out with his biological sons and Kody never met his grand-parents. Kody's godparents were Ray Charles and his wife Della; he visited them occasionally and they bought him presents.

Kody was initiated into the Crips in 1975 when he was 11. For his initiation, he and another gang member went out to steal a car, and after drinking beer and smoking pot, the gang gave Kody a beating. The group then armed itself with guns and went out looking for members of the rival gang, the Bloods. Kody was given a pump-ac-tion sawed-off shotgun and told to be sure to fire all eight shots. He did. Back home in bed that night, Kody felt guilty and ashamed of himself. He could find no reason to have shot the other gang members and he slept little that night. However, he reports feeling very little guilt thereafter.

---

[*] Kody's mother divorced Scott in 1969 when Kody was about five years old. His two older siblings also had different fathers.

After his initiation, Kody became caught up in gang life, a life that he describes as being very much like a war. In time, almost all of his energy was spent marking the gang's territory, planning attacks on rivals and committing crimes to get cars, guns and money. Walking, bicycling and riding around his area of the city became like a journey through the jungles of Vietnam, knowing that the enemy might be lurking around any corner. After sixth grade, Kody stopped attending school and gang activities became a full-time job.

When he was 13, a man that Kody was robbing fought back and hit him. Kody stomped the man almost to death and left him disfigured. This earned him the nickname "Monster," a name he tried to live up to by being even more vicious in his activities. At the age of 14, Kody fired six shots at a chili dog stand where a kid worked who had hit him in public. Kody was arrested and sentenced to two months in juvenile hall, of which he served only 19 days.

Initially, the gang wars were between the Crips and the Bloods, but soon the groups started fighting among themselves and the Crips' internal battles became just as deadly as those with the Bloods. Kody was arrested continually, sometimes for crimes he committed and sometimes for ones he did not. He spent a lot of time in jail and prison, moving up through the system from juvenile facilities to adult prisons. While incarcerated, the gang members kept their gang identities and so the battles continued while they were behind bars. Members of the same gang tried to maintain contact with one another for protection.

In 1979, Kody met a woman named Tamu who had a regular job and did not use drugs or alcohol. Although their interests were different, they liked each other and began dating. In July 1980, Tamu gave birth to their daughter. On the day of the birth, Kody began the drive to the hospital to be there for the delivery, but after he had stolen a car, he intentionally drove through enemy territory, stopped near an enemy gang member and shot him three times in the chest. He then drove back home. He had chosen gang life over family life.

Although Kody's mother hated his involvement in the gang, she never threw him out of the house and she was always there when he needed her. Some gang members' mothers supported the gang's activities. One day, the mother of a gang member called Kody on the telephone; her son had been killed by enemy gang members and she wanted revenge. She went with the gang to the house of the girl who had set her son up and fired six rounds into it. And she specifically requested that the Crips murder her son's killers.

As with many organized criminal groups, there were rules that the gang members followed. Typically, civilians (that is, non-gang youths) were not supposed to be killed. Furthermore, family members were to be left in peace. Once, when a Crips' sister was raped and killed, the gang found one of the perpetrators, killed him, chopped off both his arms, left one in the street and hid the other. Family members were no longer assaulted in that neighborhood.

In late 1980, at the age of 16, Kody was arrested for murder. Though he had recently committed a murder, he was arrested and tried for one he had not committed. Interestingly, after being found not guilty in June 1981, Kody's reaction was an urgent need to shoot someone. He drove around until he saw three Bloods leaning against a car, drinking beer. He emptied his gun into them, went home and slept well.

Kody's next arrest was in 1981 for an armed robbery that he did not commit. He received a four-year sentence in a youth training school. There he met a black Muslim, Muhammad Abdullah, who initiated Kody's movement away from the gang. When he was paroled in March 1984, Kody was met by his mother and Tamu. He moved in with Tamu, but soon began to sell drugs to earn money. Muhammad kept in touch with Kody and took him to several meetings of the Muslims. In September, though, Kody was arrested again, this time for attempted murder.

While he was in prison, Kody learned that the Crips and the Bloods had decided to change direction. Each had a constitution and a program that was directed toward unifying the subordinate groups and focusing their anger on the prison system in particular and whites in general. Kody became interested and joined the new Consolidated Crip Organization (CCO).* He learned Kiswahili, the "African" language they spoke, and the rules and customs of the group. For example, they used the term "Afrikan" rather than "Black." After being sentenced to a seven-year term, Kody ended up in Folsom Prison. He continued his involvement in African-American affairs and Muhammad still kept in touch with him. Eventually, the Folsom CCO group disintegrated and Kody joined the New Afrikan Independence Movement. It took him three years to distance himself from the gangs and to be viewed as a "civilian," but he persevered.

---

* This was partly under pressure. Kody was told that if he did not join, he would be killed. The gang leaders felt that he had damaged the Crip Nation too much in the past and could not be allowed to do so in the future.

After being paroled in November 1988, Kody returned home and began to lead a straight life. He started work as a file clerk and then got a job as a security guard. He eventually moved in with Tamu again. But this did not last long.

In 1991, Kody was back in prison with a seven-year sentence for auto theft and assault. He tells us that the charges were a result of his attack on a drug dealer who refused to stop dealing on the street where Kody lived. At the time Kody wrote his autobiography, he had been in solitary confinement for three years.

Comment

It is not unusual that Kody joined a gang; many young boys in his section of Los Angeles did just the same thing. As well, growing up in such an alienating family environment made companionship very important and as a young boy, the gang offered him that. Gang membership also gave him status, financial protection and sexual gratification. In fact, if Kody had not joined, it would have been considered a deviant act. He was what criminologists call a subcultural delinquent, a delinquent who does what his peers do. Interestingly, as he matured, Kody swapped one subculture (the Crips) for another (the New Afrikan Movement), but he continued to conform.

Reference

Scott, K. *Monster.* New York: Atlantic Monthly Press, 1993.

Chapter 16

Felons Who Murder

Murder is often committed in the context of felonious acts. Armed robbers sometimes murder the people they are robbing, contract and revenge murders occur and sexual offenders may murder their victims. In Detroit from 1970 to 1978, Dietz (1983) found that about 28 percent of the homicides were felony homicides and some of these met the definition of serial murder.

Dietz noted that felony murders were characterized by impersonality and profit motivation and often involved groups of killers and witnesses. The role of "killer" was often accepted by the criminal as part of his self-concept and, in the extreme case of the professional killer, became an important part of his identification both personally and by others.

To illustrate robbery-murder, Dietz interviewed "David" whose group committed over 200 robberies and rapes and six robbery-murders. David began his criminal behavior when he was 12 along with his friends Donald, Dwayne, Albert and LeRoy. At first they did not plan their crimes. Each would socialize with his own group of friends, then get together at 2 a.m. and drive around until they spotted a suitable victim or house to rob. Although their robberies required little planning, Donald was the one with "ideas" and Dwayne followed Donald's lead. Donald did the driving, supplied the weapons and decided how the loot would be split. If the victims included women, David and Dwayne would rape them. The group killed if the victims threatened them and David told Dietz that the way the victims looked and acted played a large role in whether they were hurt. Afterwards, they relaxed and talked about their crimes, even if the victims had been killed. On one occasion, Dwayne beat an old man to death and Donald teased him about it. In many of their killings, they would plan to strangle or bludgeon the victims, but too many of the victims struggled and so the group turned to guns. Donald committed most of the murders in this group.

In the sex murders, the victims were typically killed in order to allow the killer to escape without detection. Dietz describes one offender who was living with his girlfriend's family. When she was out one day, he asked her father for the keys to the car and, when the father refused, he killed him with hammer blows. He then took a knife from the kitchen and tried to rape his girlfriend's sister. She tried to escape and he stabbed her, her brother and a baby to death. The victims were killed because they had thwarted him.

In another case, 15-year-old Wade, whose criminal career had begun when he was nine years old—including car theft, breaking-and-entering and murder—decided with his 17-year-old friend Milo, to rob an 83-year-old woman in the neighborhood. After they broke in, Wade dragged the old lady to her bedroom and started to rape her. Milo complained, reminding Wade that they had come for money. Wade asked the woman where her money was hidden, but she would not tell him. He tied her up with telephone cords, hit her several times and put a sheet over her head. She did not survive.

Dietz gives several examples of contract killings. In one case, Henry (who was responsible for at least six contract killings) had been asked to kill two women and a man. He took his son and his son's friend along with him. He planned to drown all three intended victims in the bathtub and to steal any money or drugs he found. When he reached the apartment, he found one of the women home, but in the company of her baby and a girlfriend (not the intended victim). Henry's group tied the two women up and waited until the second intended victim arrived home from work at two in the morning. After she had been tied up, the man arrived, but as the offenders were trying to subdue him, he escaped through the apartment window. Henry fired at him as he fled, then shot the three women.

Henry took care to calm his victims as they waited for the next person to arrive. He did this by making them believe that they were safe and that it was the person expected who was in trouble. He had not planned on using his gun because the neighbors might hear the noise. Once the man escaped and the first shot had been fired, then the executions had to be completed quickly so that escape was possible. The disruption in plans also impeded the robbery of the apartment, but that was a side issue since Henry was being paid $8000 for the executions.

Henry depersonalized his victims by referring to them as "two girls" and by forgetting their names. He also had forgotten how many shots were fired and whether he had killed all three victims or whether his son's friend had killed one.

Henry was first approached about killing for pay when he was in prison. He talked it over with his wife when he got out, but she thought he was not suited for that kind of work. However, when he was offered his first contract, money was short and his wife agreed and eventually helped her husband. Henry's personality was ideal for the work. He was cool, unafraid and efficient. When Henry's son was 17, Henry and his wife took him along on a kill. Henry sent his wife outside the store where the killings were to occur, but had his son watch him. In this first experience for his son, Henry had him steal some cigarettes and empty the cash register while he killed the victims. Eventually, Henry allowed his son to have contact with the victims and to restrain them.

Ressler and co-workers (1983) reported the case of a 24-year-old offender, the youngest of three children. Because he was an Rh baby, he was given a complete blood transfusion and had no further health problems. The parents divorced when he was seven and he lived with his mother. Her second marriage ended when he was 12. He left high school in his senior year because of absenteeism and poor performance.

The boy's misbehavior was first recorded at the age of nine when he wrote swear words on the sidewalk. However, when he was 12, his misbehavior increased in seriousness when he began committing petty larceny and driving a stolen car without a license. He also began using alcohol and drugs. At the age of 14, he broke into a neighboring apartment, raped the woman there several times[*] and stole property worth about $100. For this crime he was sentenced to an out-of-state psychiatric center for 18 months by a female judge.

After coming back home, the boy raped two women and gang-raped two others with friends. When he was 17, he attempted to rape a woman, but she escaped. He was arrested for this attack but charged with armed robbery. During the year he spent waiting for the case to come to trial, he committed the first of five rape-murders. He was eventually placed on probation for the "armed robbery" and arrested eight months later for the rape-murders.

The boy weighed about 140 pounds and was 5 feet 6 inches tall. Diagnosed as having an adolescent adjustment reaction, a character

---

[*] He typically raped his victims several times because he could not ejaculate.

disorder without psychosis and multiple personality, he was judged sane, found guilty and given a life sentence for the murders.

For the rape-murders, this offender selected his victims at random, and these were mostly women from the apartment complex where he lived. He would typically catch them in an elevator, take out a knife and announce that it was a holdup. He tried to subdue the women verbally, but if that failed he used physical force. He committed the rapes either in his car or at a location near the apartment complex. The first murder victim tried to escape after being raped. He chased her into a ravine, caught her in an armlock, hit her head against a rock and held her head under a pool of water until she was dead. The second murder victim also tried to run away after the rape, but he chased her and killed her by stabbing her 14 times. In general, victims who tried to run away were killed, as were victims who made him afraid that they recognized him and might have him arrested. (Interestingly, the police did not consider the crimes to be rape-murders since no semen was detected on examination of the victims.)

Ressler argued that the murders were committed primarily to escape arrest and not for the pleasure of killing itself. Although the first murders were committed after the victims tried to escape, in subsequent cases the offender made the decision to murder the victims before he committed the rapes.

Comment

Felons who murder are not usually found to have a serious psychiatric disturbance. They probably would be diagnosed as having a chronic maladaptive lifestyle and most likely an antisocial personality disorder. Like gang members who kill, they appear to be subcultural criminals and their criminal behavior is accepted and considered a means to achieve status. As the seriousness of the criminal behavior escalates, the possibility that victims will be harmed and killed increases and some of the felons do eventually become serial murderers.

References

Dietz, M.L. *Killing for Profit.* Chicago: Nelson-Hall, 1983.
Ressler, R.K., A.W. Burgess and J.E. Douglas. Rape and rape-murder. *American Journal of Psychiatry* 140:36-40, 1983.

Chapter 17

Murders Disguised as Medical Deaths

Occasionally a series of what appear to be natural deaths later turn out to be the work of a serial killer. Two common types of this kind of act involve staff members who kill a series of patients in a hospital or nursing home and family members who kill other family members.

Hospital Murders

There are several known cases in which a series of patients at hospitals or nursing homes were killed by staff. One such case was reported in Toronto, Canada (Buehler et al., 1985); interestingly, the prime suspect was never charged with the crime and, as of this writing, still remains free.

The hospital where this happened is a 700-bed, university-affiliated hospital. In April 1980, the cardiology unit was enlarged to include two adjacent wards and a central nursing station. Physicians were assigned to either four- or six-week rotations, and the nurses worked in teams, one team for each ward, with 12-hour shifts. Each team had four to five nurses. Other personnel also worked on the wards, including intravenous phlebotomy staff, special therapists, nursing instructors and ward clerks, but they did not typically work after 10 o'clock at night. All medicines were prepared by the nurses and they also administered all oral medications. Physicians gave the intravenous medications (except for antibiotics). Patients who required the medication digoxin received it orally, in the mornings between 5:30 and 9:00 and in the evenings at 9:00. Prior to March 1981, the digoxin was kept on open shelves in the ward medication rooms.

After an epidemic of deaths on the unit and the arrest of one nurse for murder, Buehler and his associates reviewed the unit's records. From January 1976 until June 1980, there were 49 deaths on the unit, with one to four deaths each quarter. Between July 1980 and March 1981, there were 34 deaths on the unit, with nine to 11 each quarter. The risk of death during this "epidemic" was about four times higher than it was previously. The death rate in other units in the hospital, however, showed no increase for this period.

Buehler reviewed several patient-care features that could have been responsible for the increase in mortality. However, he found no changes in the occupancy rate for the unit (especially the intensive care unit), in the number of cardiac catheterizations and surgeries, the duration of surgical procedures, the nurse-to-patient ratio, the pattern of physician assignments and routines for delivery of medications and food.

Buehler then compared the patients who died during the epidemic with those who died prior to and after the epidemic. The deaths during the epidemic were more likely to occur in patients who were under one year of age (92 percent versus 50 percent). Focusing on infants under one year of age, those infants who died during the epidemic were more likely to begin the death process between midnight and 6:00 a.m. (79 percent versus 0 percent) and to actually die during this time period (76 percent versus 10 percent). The infants who died during the epidemic were more likely to die on the ward rather than in the intensive care unit (94 percent versus 60 percent), to be on Ward A rather than Ward B (82 percent versus 14 percent), to have an indwelling intravenous line (91 percent versus 60 percent), and were less likely to have a "do not resuscitate" order (6 percent versus 50 percent).

Autopsies were performed on 26 of the 33 infants who died during the epidemic and six of the 10 infants who died at other times. The consultant pathologist found almost all of the deaths understandable given the anatomical findings. Most of the children had serious heart defects. However, a consultant cardiologist found 76 percent of the epidemic deaths to be unexpected, compared to only 30 percent of the other deaths.

A consultant pharmacologist reviewed clinical and forensic digoxin measurements for the infant deaths during the epidemic. Seven patients were not assessed for digoxin. Seven of the remaining 24 patients received high scores for possible digoxin poisoning and four of these patients were judged likely to have died as the result of a single dose of digoxin given intravenously two hours prior to death. However, none of these had been prescribed a dose of digoxin in the four hours prior to death and only one had been prescribed digoxin in the eight hours prior to death, and this was orally administered.

Buehler then examined the association between the staff and the infant deaths during the epidemic. Because physicians were assigned to the unit for only four or six weeks, no physician was associated with the occurrence of the infant deaths. Four nurses were associated with high numbers of the infant deaths: Nurse A with 31, Nurse B with 22, Nurse C with 21 and Nurse D with 18. Infant deaths were 64 percent more likely to occur when Nurse A was on duty, eight times more likely when Nurse B was on duty, seven times more likely when Nurse C was on duty and five times more likely when Nurse D was on duty. Nurse B was originally arrested for the murders (on March 25, 1981), but was fully exonerated and later released.

When the results as well as other evidence were presented to a Royal Commission of Inquiry, the presiding judge concluded that eight deaths were due to digoxin poisoning and 15 others were suspicious. He regretted the arrest of Nurse B, but no other arrest has ever been made by the police.[*] However, digoxin has been declared a controlled substance at the hospital and stored in locked cabinets.

A Mother Allegedly Kills Her Children

Toufexis (1994) reported the case of a mother in New York State who was charged with murdering five of her children. Waneta Hoyt, 47, lost her first child 30 years ago. When her baby was three months old, she told doctors that she found him barely breathing in his crib and could not revive him. A second son died suddenly at the age of two and another daughter choked on her food and died when she was only 48 days old. The next daughter died in her bed at three months as did her last-born child, a son. All the deaths were classified as natural deaths. After these losses, the Hoyts adopted a son who is now 17 years old. Mrs. Hoyt grieved for her children, kept photographs of them in her house and laid flowers on their graves every Memorial Day.

A pediatrician was intrigued by the last two deaths and compiled

---

[*] Personal communication from Dr. James Buehler, March 29, 1994.

the case history of the children in this family (published in the medical journal *Pediatrics* in 1972) as an example of how sudden infant death syndrome (SIDS) can run in a family, suggesting a possible genetic component.

In April 1994, Mrs. Hoyt was charged with murdering her five children by suffocating them—three with pillows, one with a towel and one by compression against her shoulder. The difficulty in identifying such murders is that murder by suffocation is very similar on autopsy to deaths from SIDS. Two clues that should alert authorities to the possibility of murder are a series of SIDS deaths in one family and a history of the mother bringing the children to the hospital barely breathing, claiming that the baby frequently loses consciousness. This does not typically happen in SIDS deaths.

It is often hypothesized that such parents suffer from a type of Munchausen's syndrome, a psychiatric disorder in which people feign or induce an illness in order to obtain attention and a caring response from doctors. In this variant, Munchausen's syndrome by proxy, the people achieve this by harming their children.

How did Mrs. Hoyt get caught? The local district attorney, William Fitzpatrick, was writing a paper on infanticide and came across the article published in *Pediatrics* on the Hoyt family. The medical examiner who gave the journal article to Fitzpatrick, Linda Norton, commented that it looked like a case of serial murder. Although the family was not mentioned by name in the article, Fitzpatrick tracked them down and he was able to use the extensive records kept by the pediatrician on the youngest two children to provide evidence that they did not die of SIDS. Mrs. Hoyt eventually confessed to the murders, but recanted her confession before being brought to trial.

In another case, Toufexis (1994) noted that between 1972 and 1985, all nine of Marybeth Twinning's children died of SIDS and other natural causes. A rare genetic defect had been suspected, even though one child was adopted, but Twinning was eventually convicted of murdering her last child in 1986.

References

Buehler, J.W., L.F. Smith, E.M. Wallace, C.W. Heath, R. Kusiak and J.L. Herndon. Unexplained deaths in a children's hospital. *New England Journal of Medicine* 313:211-216, 1985.

Toufexis, A. When is crib death a cover for murder? *Time* 143(15): 63-64, April 11, 1994.

Chapter 18

Satanic Serial Murder

It is frequently suggested in the press that satanic cults engage in serial murder, sacrificing victims as part of their rituals. Is there any validity in this?

Lanning (1989) urged that caution be exercised in discussing this issue. Commenting on the recent flood of law enforcement seminars and conferences on satanism, he noted that the typical conference covers such topics as the history of satanism and witchcraft, fantasy role-playing games such as Dungeons and Dragons, the lyrics of heavy metal music, teenage "stoner" gangs, teenage suicide, crimes committed by self-labeled satanic practitioners, ritualistic abuse of children and conspiracies (such as claims that satanists have infiltrated established organizations and agencies). Lanning viewed most of this material as sheer nonsense.

He noted that many of those who inveigh against satanism label any religious belief other than their own as "satanic." After all, the Ayatollah Khomeini, the spiritual leader of Iran in the 1980s, referred to the United States as the "Great Satan" because America was not Muslim. Lanning recited a litany of groups and practices that have been labeled by some as satanic: demonology, witchcraft, Santeria, voodoo, Rosicrucians, Freemasonry, Knights Templar, heavy metal and rock music, the KKK, Nazis, Scientology, the Unification Church, the Way, Hare Krishna, astrology, transcendental meditation, holistic medicine, Buddhism, Hinduism, Mormonism, Islam, the Eastern Orthodox Church and Roman Catholicism. Clearly, those who fear satanism take the issue to extremes.

"Occult" means hidden or secret and usually refers to matters involving the action or influence of the supernatural. It does not imply wrong-doing or evil. "Ritualistic" refers to any customarily repeated act or series of actions. For example, Thanksgiving and Christmas ceremonies are rituals, as are the initiation ceremonies of fraternities and sororities, gangs and social clubs. Criminal acts can also involve rituals because the crimes follow a pattern—a *modus operandi*. For example, some burglars routinely urinate and defecate on the floor of the houses they enter. People diagnosed with obsessive-compulsive disorder may feel compelled to perform certain actions that they cannot stop repeating. Such behavior is often ritualistic. Some psychotic patients also exhibit ritualistic behavior. Serial murders may be ritualistic, but that in itself does not make them satanistic.

Lanning then asked what could make a crime deserve the label satanic. It cannot be that the offender belongs to a satanic church, for then a murder by a Christian would be a "Christian murder." It cannot be the discovery of symbols in the offender's home, for then the presence of a bible or crucifix would make the criminal acts of the owner Christian crimes. What about the presence of symbols at the crime scene, the bizarreness or cruelty of the crime (such as mutilation of the victim), the timing of the act (such as on Halloween), or the fact that the offender claims that Satan told him to commit the crime? Lanning suggested that the motivation of the crime be used as the criterion, but noted that occasional criminal behavior is motivated by Christian principles, such as the bombing of abortion clinics and the murder of doctors who perform abortions. The medieval Crusades and the modern civil wars in Ireland, India and Lebanon all involve crimes committed in the name of organized religions.

Lanning conceded that some people who hold satanistic beliefs do commit crimes, but the issue is whether the beliefs *caused* the crimes or whether some other causal factor led to both satanic beliefs and the criminal behavior, such as low self-esteem. Finally, Lanning suggested the following definition of a satanic murder: the murder must be rationally planned and the prime motivation must be the fulfillment of a prescribed satanic ritual that calls for the murder. However, he was unable to find a single murder in America which fit his definition.

Despite Lanning's words of caution, other writers claim that satanic serial murderers absolutely do exist. For example, Terry (1987) argues that the serial murders committed by David Berkowitz ("Son of Sam") in New York City in 1976 and 1977 and others across America were the product of a satanic network known as the Process Church. Newton (1993) estimated that 8 percent of American serial murderers confessed to or had occult motives in their crimes. He mentions several: Robert Berdella who killed six men in Kansas City, Missouri, in the 1980s and possessed books on witchcraft and a satanic robe; James and Susan Carson who murdered three people in the 1980s in California in the name of Allah; Antone Costa who murdered four women in Cape Cod in the 1970s and stocked his prison cell with books on ritual magic; Thomas Creech who confessed to 47 murders in the 1960s and 1970s in the west and claimed that some were sacrifices for a satanic cult (though authorities doubt this); Joseph Danks who murdered five transients in Los Angeles' Koreatown in the 1980s and claimed to be a pagan fighting the Christians; Larry Eyler who killed 23 young men and boys in the midwest and mutilated some of his victims with ritualistic signs and buried four in a barn marked with an inverted pentagram; Vaughn Greenwood who murdered 11 people on Skid Row in Los Angeles in the 1960s and 1970s and left cups of blood and rings of salt around the corpses; Donald Harvey who killed 87 patients in hospitals and admitted to being fascinated with black magic; Leonard Lake who, along with Charles Ng, murdered some 25 people in the 1980s and was, according to his wife, affiliated with a coven of witches; Bobby Joe Maxwell who stabbed nine homeless victims on Skid Row in Los Angeles in the 1970s and scrawled the name of Satan in blood near one of the victims; Wayne Nance, a truck driver from Montana, who worshipped Satan and was suspected of five murders; William Schmidt who was suspected of at least four murders in the 1980s, including two wives, and who belonged to the mystic Osirian Order; and Michael Swango, a physician in Illinois, who was suspected of killing patients in a hospital and who possessed occult paraphernalia.

Looking at this list does confirm some of Lanning's warnings reviewed above. The so-called satanic killers include people who are Muslim and those who call themselves pagans. Some merely owned books on witchcraft, but one (omitted from the list above) was described by Newton as a "professional magician."

Kahaner (1988) is also convinced that satanic crime exists, and believes that sometimes it extends to serial murder. Richard Ramirez, the California "Night Stalker" who was charged with 13 murders in 1985, proclaimed his ties to satanism and had a pentagram tattooed on his left palm. Hickey (1991) noted several other serial murderers who seem to have dabbled in the occult, such as Henry Lucas who supposedly kidnapped children to be used for human sacrifices and prostitution in the period 1976 to 1982.

A Possible Case of Satanic Murder

Ivey (1993a) defined satanism as a charismatic cult religion that blasphemously inverts traditional Christian beliefs. It has a codified shared supernatural belief system, a high level of social cohesiveness, strong influence over members by the group's norms, and the imputation of divine power to the group or its leaders. (Note that Lanning would object to this definition for, by analogy, it would force us to label some crimes as "Christian.") Like any religion, satanism provides the following attractive features for its members: absolute, unambiguous and simple answers to the meaning of life; instant community identity and a relief from alienation and loneliness; and emotional energy and excitement leading to euphoria. However, in addition, satanism provides permission for the gratification of desires normally considered taboo, especially sexual and aggressive desires; it legitimates rebellion against the traditional society; and to some it seems to be a more powerful ideology than Christianity. Ivey noted that several life experiences seem to predispose people to join satanic cults, including the emotional withdrawal of parents, exposure to family violence, marital separation or divorce and psychological disturbance in the parents.

Ivey (1993b) presented the case of Robert, a middle-aged businessman from Johannesburg, South Africa. He had joined a satanist church when he was 22, was an active member for eight years and then converted to Christianity. As a child, Robert was abused by his father, both verbally and physically. The father was an alcoholic who frequently beat his wife and, on one occasion, beat and raped Robert's younger sister. Robert remembered telling his mother when he was a child that one day he would murder his father. Robert described himself as an intelligent, artistic, quiet and introverted child.

One night when Robert was 14, his father returned home drunk and began to beat his wife. Robert picked up a knife, walked into his parents' bedroom and thrust the knife into his father's chest. The father survived, but as he was carried out on a stretcher, Robert heard a voice inside him saying, "I can give you power over life and death," a voice Robert later identified as Satan's.

After the father's recovery, the parents divorced and Robert's academic performance began to decline. He developed stomach ulcers by the age of 15, but he managed to finish school and went to college to study business administration. He was caught up in the spirit of the 1960s, started using drugs, eventually became an international drug dealer and then joined a satanist church in 1969.

Robert reported visitations from Satan, who he described as a seven-foot-tall, black-robed figure who assigned him the role of killing people. Robert then became a hit man for his drug-dealing acquaintances and he killed people who tried to leave the church or expose its illegal activities. When interviewed by Ivey, it still amused Robert to remember the facial expressions on the people he killed. He claimed to be able to kill people by simply cursing them. Satan gave him confidence and a powerful sense of control, pride and exhilaration, especially since Satan had appeared to him personally.

Robert claimed to have experienced possession by a number of lesser spirits, especially Asmodeus who transformed him into a violent, powerful, aggressive person who attacked anyone who presented even the slightest offense. Asmodeus enabled Robert to have sexual intercourse for five hours continuously without losing his erection. He felt that he had developed the mentality of Satan and that Satan was reincarnated inside him.

Not surprisingly, Robert's involvement in these activities began to destroy his personal life. Both his first and second wives divorced him when they learned of his secret side. When he tried to leave his church, however, he was physically assaulted. He appealed to God to protect him and two weeks later God appeared to Robert, an experience that he says transformed his life.

Ivey analyzes Robert's experiences in psychological terms. Robert's father was a violent, unloving person, yet Robert probably identified with him as most sons do with their fathers. Robert internalized a "bad" parent. This "bad" part of Robert's mind split off, became dissociated and appeared to Robert as a hallucination of Satan. (This process is called *projection* in Freud's psychoanalytic theory.) When Robert became possessed by "evil spirits," the internalized "bad" parent assumed control of his mind. As a result, Robert acted violently in the same way that his father did. Similarly, his father drank and Robert took drugs—like father, like son.

Robert's rebellion—adopting the 1960s culture, engaging in illegal activities, hating authority figures such as the police and being attracted to satanism—are all the result of Robert's conscious, intense hatred of his father. Robert identified with this "bad" father (thereby acting like him in some ways) while also rebelling against authority figures (symbolic fathers).

Interestingly, Robert must also have identified with a "good" parent, perhaps his mother. As such, a part of his mind also split off with this theme, a theme which he was able to externalize as the Christian God in one of his hallucinations, an experience which effected his conversion from satanism to Christianity.

References

Ivey, G. The psychology of Satanic worship. *South African Journal of Psychology* 23:180-185, 1993a.

Ivey, G. Psychodynamic aspects of demonic possession and Satanic worship. *South African Journal of Psychology* 23:186-194, 1993b.

Hickey, E.W. *Serial Murderers and Their Victims*. Pacific Grove, CA: Brooks/Cole, 1991.

Kahaner, L. *Cults That Kill*. New York: Warner Books, 1988.

Lanning, K.V. Satanic, occult, ritualistic crime. *Police Chief* 56(1):62-83, 1989.

Newton, M. *Raising Hell*. New York: Avon Books, 1993.

Terry, M. *The Ultimate Evil*. Garden City, NY: Doubleday, 1987.

Chapter 19

Psychiatric Disturbance in Serial Murderers

One critical issue regarding serial murderers is whether they are psychiatrically disturbed and in what way. There are two separate issues here. The first, and the one more commonly heard about in the popular media, is whether a murderer is sane or not, that is, whether he is competent to stand trial and whether he is guilty *and* insane (or not guilty through reason of insanity—the label depends upon the jurisdiction).

The legal arguments tend to upset scholarly psychologists and psychiatrists because "experts" line up for the defense and for the prosecution and often argue illogically and unscientifically for both sides of the case. Ullman (1992) attended the trial of Jeffrey Dahmer, tried in 1992 for the slaughter of 17 victims in Milwaukee, and hoped to that she would not be subject to the embarrassment she had experienced at previous trials in which insanity was used as a defense. She was disappointed. She watched the expert witnesses try to project themselves as competent authorities, but she heard them utter such inanities as that Dahmer found the killings "distasteful," despite the fact that he admitted tenderizing and sautéing parts of the hearts, biceps and thigh muscles of several victims *out of curiosity*. She heard Dahmer diagnosed as having paraphilia (a general term for sexual deviation), necrophilia (attraction to dead bodies), alcoholism, an unspecified personality disorder and an antisocial personality disorder (which has largely replaced the term psychopath). Ullman concluded that "the numbing mumbo jumbo was certainly impairing my mind. I also wondered if the doctors' 50 to 80 or more hours of evaluation had turned them into...zombies...." (p. 30).

In this chapter, therefore, I want to avoid the legal issue of sanity and focus instead on the psychiatric diagnosis given to the serial murderer, regardless of the implication of this diagnosis for criminal justice issues (guilty versus not guilty and type of sentence). I will review two cases: one the case of a serial murderer who was interviewed by a psychiatrist twice after conviction and who was judged to be psychotic, and the other a case of a serial murderer who claimed to have a multiple personality but who was judged to be faking it by the evaluating psychiatrist.

Joseph Kallinger: A Psychotic Killer

Joseph Kallinger was born in 1936 to a 19-year-old mother. Joseph was the result of an affair after she was separated from her husband (Areti and Schreiber, 1981; Schreiber, 1983). She nursed Joseph for a month and then gave him up for adoption. He was placed with the Kallingers when he was 22 months old. The Kallingers were cruel to Joseph. They fed and clothed him well, but they constantly reminded him that they had rescued him from an orphanage and that he owed them everything. Whenever he misbehaved, they threatened to send him back to the orphanage.

Joseph had an operation for a hernia when he was six and a half. After the operation the Kallingers told him that the surgeon had fixed his penis so that it would never grow and never get hard. The doctor, they told him, had delivered Joseph from evil and now Joseph would be a "good boy." The Kallingers were physically and psychologically cruel in many other ways. They punished Joseph by making him kneel for hours on coarse sandpaper; they burned his fingers on the gas stove; they hit him on the head with hammers; they flogged him with a cat-of-nine-tails. They overprotected him and isolated him from other children. They called him a coward when he was attacked by the other children and did not fight back. When he was eight, he was sexually assaulted by three boys who held a knife to his throat.

Joseph's disturbed behavior was apparent by the age of 12. He cut a hole in his bedroom wall and, while masturbating in the hole, would stab the breasts in pictures of nude women. A year later he lured a boy to a secluded area and forced him to strip with the goal of castrating him. He fled instead. He began to develop fantasies about knives being used for aggressive and sexual purposes.

The Kallingers grew scared of their son and allowed him to move out and rent a furnished room. Surprisingly, at the age of 16, he married a local girl who soon left him for another man. Joseph remarried and had five children. Mr. Kallinger had trained Joseph as a shoemaker and he functioned well as a provider and parent. But Joseph's psychosis began to interfere with his life. He dug a hole in the ground under his warehouse and, when he felt the episodes of madness engulfing him, he would go there until the feeling passed.

In 1972, Joseph burned his daughter and was sentenced to eight months in prison for child abuse; there he was diagnosed as schizophrenic. After his return home, Joseph began to believe that he was God and became determined to kill every living human. He allied himself with one of his sons (one who had turned him over to the police for child abuse) and began his serial murders.[*] In 1973, Joseph and his son began taking bus trips to the suburbs where they would choose a house for the son to break into and burglarize. Soon Joseph joined the son in breaking and entering. They killed and mutilated a young boy in July 1974, and soon thereafter drowned one of Joseph's other sons. Although they broke into several houses intending to kill the occupants, Joseph often could not bring himself to do so. Finally, in January 1975, there were seven potential victims in a house they had broken into. He ordered a woman there to bite off the penis of one of the men and, when she refused, he stabbed her to death. Joseph was arrested nine days later for the murders and break-ins. He had three trials and he was found guilty each time. Since 1978, Joseph has been in an institution for the criminally insane in Pennsylvania.

Arieti examined Joseph twice, once in 1980 and again in 1981. In 1980, Joseph was subdued, but not apathetic. He was on medication that reduced his anxiety. However, he complained that the medication diminished his hallucinations and fantasies—the life inside his mind which was so important to him. He reported that in 1969 he started hearing voices that told him to carve holes in people so that he could insert his penis and to kill them. He would sometimes ejaculate while hearing the voices. Prior to 1972, he thought that the voices were from the Devil, but after 1972 he came to believe they were from God. He felt that God would give him the power to destroy the whole of mankind.

---

[*] Joseph thought that this son had the biggest penis in the family. This son was also the child least liked by the mother, which may have led him to ally himself with his father.

Arieti judged that Joseph was still hallucinating and delusional. He also manifested stereotyped and rhythmic body movements and used a private language. Arieti diagnosed Joseph as a paranoid schizophrenic.

Arieti visited Joseph a year later. He was friendlier and more alert on this visit and was able to answer general knowledge questions much better, perhaps as a result of a change in medication recommended by Arieti on the previous visit. Joseph still talked about his hallucinations and delusions. He told Arieti that God had ordered him to commit the criminal acts—a God who looked and dressed just like Joseph. There was also a character called Charlie—a disembodied head—who talked to Joseph. Just the month before, God had ordered Joseph to kill another inmate, but he had managed to resist.

Arieti concluded that Joseph's psychosis was still active and that the diagnosis of paranoid schizophrenia was still appropriate.

Did the Hillside Strangler Have a Multiple Personality?

Kenneth Bianchi and his cousin Angelo Buono tortured, raped and murdered 10 women in Los Angeles from 1977 to 1978. After Bianchi moved to Bellingham, Washington, the Los Angeles murders stopped, but two women were murdered in Bellingham and Bianchi was arrested for these murders and tried for all 12. Bianchi tried to convince authorities that he suffered from multiple personality disorder, a defense which had become popular as a way of seeking a verdict of "not guilty through reason of insanity." He eventually abandoned that strategy and agreed to testify against Buono as part of a plea bargain.

While awaiting trial, Bianchi was interviewed by six mental health professionals. Some were prepared to argue for the defense that Bianchi had a multiple personality and others were prepared to argue for the prosecution that he was faking the disorder. Orne and co-workers (1984) published a report of an evaluation that was conducted for the prosecutors and which in part led Bianchi's lawyers to drop the insanity defense and instead to plea bargain.

Bianchi was adopted at the age of three months and had behavioral disorders from an early age. He wet the bed until he was 11 and, though his mother took him to many urologists, the bed-wetting did not stop until she began to work outside the home. He may have been severely disciplined and perhaps abused by his mother and he showed great ambivalence toward her. He seems to have lied persistently from an early age. Although his IQ was found to be 116 when tested in prison, he performed poorly at school. As a child, Bianchi seemed to fall easily and a physician diagnosed petit mal epilepsy when he was five. However, testing in prison revealed no obvious brain damage. He was evaluated at the age of 11 because of absenteeism at school, tics, bed-wetting and asthma; although psychotherapy was recommended, his mother declined to take him for treatment. His adoptive father died when Bianchi was 13.

As an adult, Bianchi wanted to be a police officer, but he was never accepted into the police academy. He had 12 different jobs, some as a security officer, in the nine years after high school. His first marriage, at the age of 19, ended after eight months and at the age of 26 he began to live with another woman. They had one child together.

Bianchi continued to commit a variety of petty crimes—shoplifting, using stolen credit cards, pimping young male prostitutes and selling drugs. In Los Angeles, he fraudulently set himself up as a psychologist, obtaining transcripts and diplomas to which he forged his name. He had a number of psychological texts, though he claimed not to understand them (this may be significant in terms of Bianchi's claim of having a multiple personality disorder).

The possibility of a second personality appeared while he was under hypnosis during initial interviews with a psychiatrist for the defense. In scientific circles, the existence of a multiple personality is not accepted if the person has been hypnotized. Hypnosis is a highly suggestible state and it is easy for a hypnotist to suggest the symptoms of a multiple personality while the patient is hypnotized. The first hypnotist also suggested to Bianchi under hypnosis that "Ken" might remember events that happened when he was "Steve," again a procedure that would disqualify the case in scientific circles. The evaluation of the case was also made difficult by the fact that Bianchi had read all of the reports prepared by experts for his defense lawyers, including medical and psychiatric reports from his childhood. He also had seen two movies on multiple personality (*Three Faces of Eve* and *Sybil*) prior to the interviews.

Orne set out to determine whether Bianchi was faking a multiple personality disorder in two ways: Was he faking the hypnotic trance and did his behavior fit the syndrome of multiple personality?

Was Bianchi Faking a Hypnotic Trance?

Orne had conducted several research studies which showed that hypnotists could not determine whether their clients were faking hypnosis or not (Orne, 1977). One test, for example, asks the hypnotized person to hallucinate a person and then introduces the real person into the room. A truly hypnotized person reports the presence of the real person, acknowledges that there are two of them, but does not appear distressed. People who are simulating hypnosis deny the presence of the double. Bianchi acknowledged the double, but continued to ask questions about the paradox in a way that truly hypnotized people do not.

In about a third of persons who are truly hypnotized, when it is suggested that they "see" someone in a chair, they will do so, but they will also report seeing the chair clearly. Bianchi did not report this. If it is suggested to truly hypnotized persons that a part of their hand is anesthetized, they tend to say they feel nothing when the "anesthetized" part is touched. Bianchi remained silent. Fourth, when information is given to hypnotized subjects, if they remember it after coming out of the trance, they forget the source of the information. Bianchi did not remember the information given to him while in the trance. Finally, Orne felt subjectively that Bianchi overacted, which is uncharacteristic of a truly hypnotized subject.

Orne felt that Bianchi failed four of the five tests, but it could be argued, based on Orne's findings, that he clearly failed only three of them.

Was Bianchi Faking a Multiple Personality?

Orne told Bianchi before hypnotizing him that the appearance of a third personality would be convincing evidence that Bianchi had a multiple personality disorder. During the first hypnotic trance with Orne, a third personality, "Billy," appeared. This does not happen with true multiple personalities. Orne also suggested prior to trance induction that the personality "Ken" ought to admit more flaws in his character rather than attributing all of the bad behaviors to "Steve." During the hypnotic trance, "Ken" admitted more flaws. (This point was not as convincing as it could have been because the defense hypnotist had already suggested during a hypnotic trance that breaking down amnesia was critical for a diagnosis of multiple personality.)

Bianchi showed none of the symptoms in his life that characterize people with multiple personality, such as profound shifts in personality and episodes of amnesia. Furthermore, the second personality was named by Bianchi as "Steve Walker," and it was found that this was the name Bianchi used in his efforts to fake his credentials as a psychologist, whereas the personality should have emerged in child-hood. Finally, as soon as Bianchi pled guilty, the symptoms disap-peared.

Psychological tests were administered to Bianchi while he was in each of the three personalities. Orne admits that there are no reliable and valid criteria for distinguishing a true multiple person-ality from a simulated one using psychological tests. However, one psychologist who had written on this problem was given Rorschach ink-blot test results from "Ken" and "Steve" and concluded that they resembled a psychopathic person faking multiple personality rather than a true multiple personality.

How Did Orne Diagnose Bianchi?

Based on Bianchi's history of behavioral symptoms from childhood onward, Orne concluded that Bianchi was probably a psychopath (i.e., that he had an antisocial personality disorder). Bianchi seems to have murdered women for sexual gratification and so would also be diagnosed with sexual sadism. It is this combination of syndromes that increased the probability that Bianchi would become a serial murderer.

Bianchi's Los Angeles murders began when his wife became pregnant and ended when his son was born. The Bellingham murders occurred when his wife was nursing their child. Orne suggests that Bianchi's rage at his mother was triggered by maternal behavior in his wife. His wife's maternal behavior decreased his sexual interest in her and his sexual desires combined with rage at his allegedly abusive mother led Bianchi to assault and murder women. This outcome was facilitated as well by his relationship with a relative who shared a similar violent tendency. Interestingly, Bianchi did not murder his mother or wife, but rather displaced the sexual and aggressive desires onto women who were strangers.

Others, such as Watkins (1984), have reviewed the same evidence and concluded that Bianchi did have a multiple personality disor-der. However, outside of forensic circles, it is critical for proof of the existence of a personality disorder that the patient *not* be hypnotized (e.g., Horton and Miller, 1972). The power of suggestion under hypnosis is so great that the disorder can easily be suggested (overtly or covertly) to the patient by the hypnotist. Thus, I tend to trust Orne's doubts about, rather than Watkins' belief in, multiple per-sonality in Bianchi.

Serial Murder as an Addiction

Gresswell (1991) has suggested that serial murder often has similar characteristics to an addictive behavior. First, addictive activities become the most important thing in the lives of serial murderers and dominates their thinking, feelings and behaviors, and this seems to be true of those who spend a great deal of time planning, carrying out and fantasizing murders.

Second, there is often conflict over the addictive behavior both within the person and between the person and others around him. Some killers, such as Henry Lucas, have asked authorities to imprison them so as to prevent them from murdering, while others have expressed feelings of revulsion and guilt after their murders.

Third, tolerance builds up so that the addicted person requires increasing amounts of the addictive activity. This appears to be the case for some serial murderers and has been documented in a group of sexual sadists (not serial murderers) examined by MacCulloch and co-workers (1983).

Fourth, unpleasant feelings occur when the addictive activity cannot be engaged in. This has not yet been looked for in serial murderers. Fifth, the effects of the addictive behavior are so powerful that, after indulging in the behavior, the person often feels miserable and has to engage in the act again at the earliest opportunity.

Sixth, even after periods of abstinence, it is easy for the addicted person to revert quickly to the earlier extreme pattern of behavior. This is frequently shown in serial murderers. Dennis Nilsen, a serial murderer of young men in England, tried to stop on two occasions but was unable to, and he returned to his modus operandi with ease.

To illustrate the addictive nature of sexual sadism, Gresswell (1991) presented the case of a man who formulated plans for the murders of at least 20 people, but failed to carry them out. He attacked two people, both of whom survived, and he was arrested. He was convicted on two counts of attempted murder and sent to an institution for the criminally insane.

The man's parents had been cold and unaffectionate and he used to fantasize as a child about ideal parents who would one day come to claim him. He developed severe acne as a teenager and was ridiculed at school; he coped with this by developing fantasies of miracle cures for his skin condition and of sadistic revenge on those who tormented him. He eventually obtained work as a salesman for which he assumed a "salesperson's persona" that protected him against loss of a sale (rejection). He saw the customer as rejecting the persona, not himself. When the man reached the age of 30, he grew upset over the fact that he had never had a girlfriend and his skin problem worsened with no hope of further treatment. His behavior now became addictive in nature. He began to act out sequences from his revenge fantasies, prowling his local area at night, spying on potential victims and opening their mail. He assembled weapons and purchased clothes he thought suitable for committing murder. These activities excited him (they had now become salient) and yet they also disturbed him so that he discussed them with his counselor to whom he had been assigned after a suicide attempt and subsequent hospitalization. As tolerance set in, the man began to take greater risks and eventually he decided that he had to actually kill someone. He attacked his first victim after being questioned by the police about an assault he had not committed, a circumstance that led him to think that if the police considered him capable of murder, maybe he was. The victim survived and two days later he attacked a second victim who also survived. He was then arrested.

Gresswell saw this case as illustrating salience, conflict and tolerance and it is likely that, had the man not been arrested, he would eventually have murdered. Gresswell found that signs of withdrawal were difficult to observe because they were confounded by the trauma of arrest and imprisonment. Relief and relapse were noted because, after institutionalization, the man relieved his feelings of anxiety and repression by rehearsing his extremely aggressive fantasies.

References

Arieti, S. and F.R. Schreiber. Multiple murders of a schizophrenic patient. *Journal of the American Academy of Psychoanalysis* 9:501-524, 1981.

Gresswell, D.M. Psychological models of addiction and the origins and maintenance of multiple murder. *Issues in Criminological and Legal Psychology* 2(17):86-91, 1991.

Horton, P. and D. Miller. The etiology of multiple personality. *Comprehensive Psychiatry* 13:151-159, 1972.

MacCulloch, M.J., P.R. Snowden, P.J.W. Wood and H.E. Mills. Sadistic fantasy, sadistic behavior and offending. *British Journal of Psychiatry* 143:20-22, 1983.

Orne, M.T. The construct of hypnosis. *Annals of the New York Academy of Science* 296:14-33, 1977.

Orne, M.T., D.F. Dinges and E.C. Orne. On the differential diagnosis of multiple personality in the forensic context. *International Journal of Clinical and Experimental Hypnosis* 32:118-169, 1984.

Schreiber, F.R. *The Shoemaker.* New York: Simon and Schuster, 1983.

Ullman, J. I carried it too far, that's for sure. *Psychology Today* 25:28-31, May/June 1992.

Watkins, J.G. The Bianchi (L.A. Hillside Strangler) case. *International Journal of Clinical and Experimental Hypnosis* 32:67-101, 1984.

Chapter 20

The Modern Serial Murderer

For the concluding case in this book on serial murderers, I thought it would be useful to present a case of a "modern" serial murderer, one from contemporary times who seems to manifest some of the typical traits of the serial murderer described in Part I of this book. Many American serial murderers have been written about extensively and also covered by television so most readers already know the details of these cases. I have, therefore, chosen a rather gruesome case of an Englishman—Dennis Nilsen, who murdered 15 or 16 people before he was caught in 1983.[*]

Dennis Nilsen was born on November 23, 1945 in Fraserburgh, a remote fishing village on the far coast of Aberdeenshire in Scotland. Nilsen's father, Olav, was a Norwegian who arrived in Scotland during World War II as a soldier in the Free Norwegian Forces. In 1942, he married a Fraserburgh resident named Betty Whyte. Shortly after they were married, Olav's absences became more common than his presences, and after the birth of Dennis' younger sister, he deserted his family completely, never to appear again. Dennis grew up with his mother, his two siblings and a grandfather who he adored and who, in turn, took great delight in the child. Indeed, Dennis' grandfather was his idol, his ultimate beloved, a love that he was never able to surpass. His death at sea when Dennis was only six was a terribly traumatic and painful experience for the boy. An open coffin was displayed in the room where Dennis and his sister were born, but neither child really understood the meaning of the death and no one bothered to explain it to them. Dennis even had a peak

---

[*] This chapter is based on biographical material in B. Masters, *Killing for Company* (London: Hodder and Stoughton), 1991.

at his grandfather's dead body in the coffin, but his mother couldn't bring herself to tell him the truth; she told him that his grandfather was only sleeping in the box. As mention of his grandfather dwindled, Dennis believed that his grandfather had simply gone off on another fishing trip, but when he realized that his grandfather would never come home again, so great were his feelings of despair that he could hardly acknowledge the immensity of his loss. Dennis himself would later attribute his crimes of murder to this one great loss.

The remainder of Nilsen's childhood was terribly lonely and he spent long hours alone staring at the sea. His mother, however, did her best to provide a nice secure home. Dennis had some friends, but was a loner and found solace in nature and he loved animals. He kept a number of pets and built a home for some pigeons, two of which he became particularly attached to. He trained them to sit on his arm. But his attachment was short-lived; a friend senselessly killed the pigeons, and again Dennis was robbed of something he loved. He couldn't fathom that others did not have the same feelings of sensitivity toward animals and was appalled at the cruelty of other boys toward small animals. Sometimes, when he found sick animals, he would kill them to prevent them from suffering any more. He would later say he killed some of his human victims for the same reason.

Nilsen remained sexually uninitiated throughout his school years. However, he became aware that he had sexual desires for other boys. He never had the nerve to make a move toward any of the boys he liked, but he did fantasize a lot—becoming particularly obsessed with a boy in a photograph in his French grammar book. He joined the army at the age of 15 and adapted well to the rigidly structured military life. He also liked the comradery that came with army life and took particular pleasure in feeling like he was "one of the boys." Despite this outward picture, he felt nagging guilt about his attraction to men. Assigned to the Army Catering Corps, Nilsen learned how to butcher skillfully and he acquired a working knowledge of animal anatomy—a skill that he put to use later on. During his postings abroad, he had sex with female prostitutes, but he never developed an attraction toward women. However, his homosexual encounters were not much more pleasurable and he considered himself to be bisexual. Nilsen made every attempt to hide his homosexuality. This inability to express and fulfil his sexual desires caused him to feel intense guilt and pain.

Perhaps because he was unable to express himself sexually

toward others, he eventually developed a disturbing fascination for his own body. One cannot say that Nilsen simply had narcissistic leanings, for his self-interest was decidedly weird. To excite himself, he would spend hours looking at himself in the mirror, positioned very still and in such a way so that he could not see his head. He would imagine that the lifeless, "dead" body he saw reflected in the mirror belonged to someone else or he would remember his grandfather's dead body.

In 1972, he fell in love with an 18-year-old private. Nilsen was overjoyed to find a friend who seemed to like his company. One of their hobbies was making movies and Nilsen's favorite drama was the one in which the private would pretend he was dead. They made many of these movies, but Nilsen ended up burning them all as he was disgusted with a love that was not reciprocal. The closest the two ever came was holding hands.

After 11 years in the army, Nilsen joined the police force in London. He liked the life of a police officer, but he missed the after-hours companionship that he had in the army. As a police officer, he was alone when off-duty and this gave him time for brooding and dangerous introspection. He began to visit gay bars, but he disliked casual sex with strangers. The conflict over his homosexuality led Nilsen to resign from the police after a year and, after several jobs as a security guard, he applied for unemployment compensation. However, the unemployment agency found a job for him as a civil servant training the unemployed for work. Nilsen's skill as a cook led to a job training hotel workers. He worked at this for eight years, though his socialist political views made him unpopular with his co-workers, especially since Nilsen was also considered long-winded and boring.

In June 1974, Nilsen brought a 17-year-old boy, David Painter, to his rented room. The boy refused Nilsen's sexual advances and fell asleep. Nilsen took photographs of the sleeping Painter, but when the boy woke up, he was frightened by the camera equipment and started fighting Nilsen. The police were called, but no charges were filed. Soon thereafter, Nilsen came to the defense of a man who was being harassed in a gay bar and to Nilsen's delight, the man, David Gallichan (nicknamed Twinkle), suggested they share an apartment. Nilsen was overjoyed to finally have the companionship that he thought this relationship would bring. They lived together for two years, despite the fact the Gallichan had numerous affairs with other men.

After they broke up, Nilsen's life was again painfully lonely and he began to drink heavily. On December 30, 1978, Nilsen brought

home an 18-year-old and, as the boy slept, Nilsen realized that in the
morning, the boy would leave and he would once again be alone.
He wanted the boy to stay whether he wanted to or not. His method
was to kill him. First, he strangled the boy, then drowned him in a
bucket of water. Nilsen lovingly bathed the boy's body, shampooed
his hair and carefully dried him. Then he placed the naked body on
his bed. He then dressed the boy's body and cuddled in bed with it.
He knew he had done something horrible and realized that he had
to get rid of the body before being discovered. By the next day, the
body had lost its rigor mortis and Nilsen hid it under the floorboards
in his apartment. After a week, he decided that he wanted to look
at the body again, and when he removed it, he noticed that it had
gotten dirty. He washed it again and then for the next day, he
alternately used the body as a mute companion and love slave. For
much of the time he suspended the body by its ankles from the
platform of his bed. He thought about butchering the body to
dispose of it, but couldn't bring himself to actually do it. He placed
it under the floorboards again and it remained there for seven
months. He finally burned it in the backyard.

The next 14 bodies were treated similarly. They were bathed,
dressed and used for company. Sex was far less important than the
companionship they provided. Between December 1979 and February 1983, Nilsen murdered 14 young men. He tried to kill seven
others, but they managed to escape. Nilsen eventually began to cut
up the bodies after they had lost their attraction for him. He
dumped some in suitcases which he placed in a shed in the garden,
dousing them with disinfectant now and then.

As the bodies accumulated under the floorboards, in the shed,
and stuffed in closets, Nilsen gave more serious thought to disposal.
He began to butcher them systematically, at first retching and then
trying to steady himself with heavy drinking. He burned six of the
dismembered bodies in the garden and, amazingly, no one grew
suspicious. On one occasion, vandals broke into his apartment and
the investigating police never realized that there were dead bodies
under the floorboards on which they were walking.

Trouble developed because his landlords found Nilsen to be a
difficult tenant. He was always arguing about tenants' rights and
writing angry letters to them. Eventually, they persuaded him to
move to a different building and Nilsen made one last funeral pyre
in the garden.

At his new apartment, Nilsen became more systematic about
disposing of the bodies. He would cut them into very small chunks

and flush them down the toilet. Some parts were boiled to make them easier to dispose of, while other pieces were hacked into fragments and placed in the trash. Eventually, the toilets in the apartment house became blocked and on Saturday, February 5, 1983, a plumber was called to clear them. He could not clear the block and a heavy-duty unit had to be brought in on Tuesday. Meanwhile, tenants were asked to not flush their toilets.

Nilsen realized that he would soon be arrested. When the plumbers climbed down into the sewer they discovered some 40 decaying chunks of graying flesh blocking the drain. Frightened that he would be caught, Nilsen snuck out late that night and retrieved as much of the flesh as he could and threw it over the garden wall. However, he was observed by neighbors. The next day, the plumbers explored further and called the police. That same day, the police went to Nilsen's apartment, smelled the decaying flesh and asked Nilsen where the rest of the bodies were. He led them to the storage places in his apartment. Nilsen was taken into custody that day. He had already tidied his office expecting that he would not return to work.

Nilsen cooperated fully with the police whose major problem was identifying the men killed by Nilsen. The trial was straightforward, especially since some of those whom Nilsen had assaulted came forward to testify. Nilsen was convicted on six charges of murder and two of attempted murder. He was sentenced to life in prison with a minimum of 25 years to be served.

In his writings, Nilsen stated that he wished he could have stopped, but that he was unable to do so. Yet he has never seemed to show genuine remorse. His behavior was not that of someone with an antisocial personality disorder, but he is probably best diagnosed as having a chronic personality disorder of some kind. His social isolation, particularly after his army service, may have contributed to Nilsen's developing an abnormal and maladaptive lifestyle.

Nilsen's childhood was traumatic, but not brutal. He killed his victims, not out of anger, but to keep them. Thus, the frustration-aggression hypothesis does not seem relevant to his behavior. Nilsen developed a fascination with death and dead bodies in his formative years and his work as a butcher in the army probably allowed this fascination to develop and facilitated the formation of deviant fantasies. Although he retched when he dismembered his first victim, Nilsen became accustomed to the task and habituated to the stench in his apartment. Thus, although the final form of his behavior seems thoroughly disgusting, it is possible to see how Nilsen could have slowly developed his rituals given the experiences of his life.

Conclusion

In this analysis of serial murder, I have pointed to the problems that I have with various research efforts and made suggestions for improvement, but I do not in any way claim to have a magic theory explaining how people can develop into serial killers. There are possible theories, but for the most part, these cannot be applied across the board. What I have tried to do throughout is to separate the facts from the myths, illuminating the knowledge we have against matters that we can only speculate on. To conclude, then, I will briefly sum up what can be determined about serial killers.

To begin with, we have learned that the typical serial murderer is very different from the typical nonserial or conventional murderer. Almost all of the serial killers identified in modern times have been white (Wayne Williams, the man who killed children in Atlanta in the 1980s, is a rare exception), whereas a significant number of nonserial murderers are African American. Unlike conventional murderers, very few serial murderers use firearms to kill their victims, opting instead for more hands-on methods such as repeated stabbing and strangulation. Serial murder does not show any sort of regional pattern, whereas nonserial murder is more common in the southern part of the United States. And unlike the conventional murderer, who doesn't hold to any specific sexual orientation, several modern serial murderers have been homosexual; this opinion, however, may be the result of the more detailed contemporary type of investigation and reporting of modern serial murderers. It is important to note, as well, that there has not yet been a study that explores the sexual orientation of nonserial killers. Serial murderers do resemble conventional murderers in a few ways, though; the majority of both types of murderers are men and their victims are frequently women and children.

It has also been asserted that serial murder is a modern phenomenon. The cases presented in this book clearly indicate that this is not so. There have always been serial murderers; the Greeks, the Romans, medieval nobility and the pirates and cutthroats of the seventeenth and eighteenth centuries all had serial killers in their midst. Because we do not have accurate counts of the crime rates of past centuries, we cannot say that serial murder is more common today than it was in earlier times. Similarly, the apparent increase in the rate of sexual serial murder in the last 30 years could partly be the result of better criminal justice practices and increased skill in law enforcement agencies. The greater amount of information we now have should not lead us to draw conclusions about long-dead killers about whom we know less. Similarly, the serial murderer is often considered an American phenomenon, but we have seen that other countries such as Great Britain and Germany have documented many cases of serial murder.

It is particularly noteworthy that the motives of serial killers seem to have changed over the years. In preindustrial times, serial murderers tended to be depraved aristocrats preying on peasants; in the industrial era, seemingly respectable middle-class men killed prostitutes, homeless boys and housemaids. Today, serial murderers are often people who exist on the margins of society, those who have failed to achieve their personal expectations, who are mainly of working- and lower-middle-class origins, and who attack middle-class victims such as college students.

Given the interest today of both the general public and social scientists in serial murder, it is surprising how poor the research on serial murder has been. Although several typologies have been proposed for serial murderers, most have focused on the sexual serial murderer and have omitted all of the "less interesting" chronic felons who are also serial murderers. Cases in which nurses and doctors have "hastened" the deaths of many patients are also frequently not considered serial murder. None of the typologies have been tested for their usefulness in classifying a sample of serial murderers. Furthermore, what proportion of serial murderers remain unclassifiable with the typology, what proportion fall into two or more categories, and how much do different researchers agree with each other's categorization of serial murderers?

Although some investigators have described the typical characteristics of small samples of serial murderers, this needs to be done for larger samples, especially samples that include all the known serial murderers in a nation and time period.

The theories of serial murder that have been proposed thus far are quite similar to those that have been proposed for conventional murder in terms of the physiological, psychological and social factors involved. None of these theories have yet been tested for validity — a process that would require collecting data relevant to a particular theory (biochemical measures, psychiatric evaluations or psychological tests) obtained from a sample of serial murderers and a comparison sample of nonserial murderers.

It would seem reasonable to assume that since serial murder is considered a more horrendous act than conventional murder, the physiology of the serial murderer must be more defective, his psychiatric state more disturbed and the psychological factors more extreme. However, there is no evidence that this is true.

We tend to believe that a catastrophic act by an individual — whether suicide, homicide or serial murder — must have been brought on by major traumatic events in the person's life or major defects in his physiological functioning. Surprisingly, this also may not be true. Natural scientists, especially those interested in what is known as chaos theory, have documented that tiny modifications in chemical and physical variables can have a major impact on the resulting process, changing the outcome drastically.

As an example, studies of severely disturbed psychiatric patients do not typically find that these people had more horrendous childhoods full of more traumatic events than the general population. Rather, very subtle differences in childhood experiences can result in one person being labeled schizophrenic while another is not. Thus, although research studies typically show that murderers have suffered more physical and psychological frustration in childhood and adolescence than nonmurderers, it does not follow that serial murderers experienced even *more* frustration when they were growing up.

In the end, we must realize that there are so many types of serial murderers that, with the present state of knowledge, it is virtually impossible to construct a solid profile of serial killers. Much more research needs to be conducted on the psychological and behavioral characteristics of serial killers, as well as the reasons why people turn to this type of murder. A scientific understanding of this sort can only be achieved through a careful and measured study of the facts — a movement past the sensationalism toward thorough study and analysis. It is my hope that this book will be seen as a step in that direction.

Index